T0383953

Cambridge Elements

Elements in Global Urban History
edited by
Michael Goebel
Graduate Institute Geneva
Tracy Neumann
Wayne State University
Joseph Ben Prestel
Freie Universität Berlin

THE CITY BEAUTIFUL AND THE GLOBALIZATION OF URBAN PLANNING

Ian Morley
*Department of History, Chinese University
of Hong Kong*

Shaftesbury Road, Cambridge CB2 8EA, United Kingdom

One Liberty Plaza, 20th Floor, New York, NY 10006, USA

477 Williamstown Road, Port Melbourne, VIC 3207, Australia

314–321, 3rd Floor, Plot 3, Splendor Forum, Jasola District Centre,
New Delhi – 110025, India

103 Penang Road, #05–06/07, Visioncrest Commercial, Singapore 238467

Cambridge University Press is part of Cambridge University Press & Assessment,
a department of the University of Cambridge.

We share the University's mission to contribute to society through the pursuit of
education, learning and research at the highest international levels of excellence.

www.cambridge.org
Information on this title: www.cambridge.org/9781009598767

DOI: 10.1017/9781009443272

© Ian Morley 2025

When citing this work, please include a reference to the DOI 10.1017/9781009443272

First published 2025

A catalogue record for this publication is available from the British Library

ISBN 978-1-009-59876-7 Hardback
ISBN 978-1-009-44323-4 Paperback
ISSN 2632-3206 (online)
ISSN 2632-3192 (print)

The City Beautiful and the Globalization of Urban Planning

Elements in Global Urban History

DOI: 10.1017/9781009443272
First published online: January 2025

Ian Morley
Department of History, Chinese University of Hong Kong

Author for correspondence: Ian Morley, ianmorley@cuhk.edu.hk

Abstract: During the past one hundred or so years, urbanists have composed grand narratives regarding the development of urban design and the international dissemination of planning models. Yet, building upon this historiography, whilst the transnational dimension of modern city planning has centred itself upon the diffusion of the British garden city, far less attention has been put upon the global reach of the American City Beautiful. Owing to the ethnocentricity of American planning history literature, thus, the chronicle of the City Beautiful has anchored itself, literally and figuratively, to the North American continent. Yet, in truth, grand American-inspired plans were implemented throughout the world; indeed, they were carried out long after the City Beautiful's popularity had waned in North America, and they were executed under a variety of cultural and political conditions.

This Element also has a video abstract:
Cambridge.org/EGUB_Morley_Abstract

Keywords: city planning, City Beautiful, Daniel Burnham, governance, modernity

ISBNs: 9781009598767 (HB), 9781009443234 (PB), 9781009443272 (OC)
ISSNs: 2632-3206 (online), 2632-3192 (print)

Contents

1 Introduction: American City Beautiful Planning and Its Place within the Study of Global Urban History

In *The Routledge Handbook of Planning History*, Carola Hein (2018a) explains that urban planning's focus and form shift over time. Change to planning's character, she notes, is an effect of political, economic, cultural, and ideological advancement. Referring to late-1800s Europe and the United States (U.S.), Hein clarifies that planning evolved because it was conceived 'as a rational, modernist pursuit for societal improvement in response to the urban ills produced by the industrial revolution' (2018a: 2). Hence, by 1900, new environmental design models facilitated low-density residential layouts, public health improvement, transportation infrastructure development, and the revitalizing of downtowns to become the fundamentals of modern city planning thinking and practice.

Generally, inquiries of urban planning examine four core themes: the make-up of built environments; the practice of planning; societal change and transformation; and, the resolution of urban problems (Weber and Crane, 2012). However, indicate Stephen Ward, Robert Freestone, and Christopher Silver (2011), there is need for those interested in the history of city planning to know of its internationalized nature. Despite planning models such as the Garden City and City Beautiful reshaping the appearance and layout of British and American settlements during the early twentieth century, they were also globally diffused.

The Cambridge Element in Global Urban History book series supplies new structures to evaluate the forces that shaped the form and meaning of built fabrics in the past. As part of this process attention is paid to Global History. It provides analytical apparatus to move/think beyond national borders so as to better know how urban places and planning practices are interconnected. Owing to urban historians traditionally focusing upon local affairs, Global History thus initiates frameworks to extend inquiry beyond the territorial confines of a particular town, city, or country (Sandoval-Strausz and Kwak, 2018).

The attitudes, methods, and findings of persons from different academic backgrounds have significance to the Element. Subsequently, an analysis is provided of how a French Beaux Arts-inspired planning model was established in the U.S. and then applied in different parts of the world. Why the City Beautiful was used in those localities, and what it meant to each nation's development, will be discussed.

Given that the Element presents City Beautiful planning in an internationalized setting, it aims to build upon the studies undertaken by scholars such as Robert Freestone (2007a and 2023), Gilbert A. Stelter (2000), and Daniel T. Rodgers (1998). Rodgers explains why by 1900, Paris, France, had become an environmental design exemplar in countries attached to the North Atlantic economy. Likewise, Stelter illuminates how with the global rise of the idea that a city could be a work of art, *the* early-1900s urban design model was Paris. Supplementing such inquiry, Freestone highlights that whilst the City Beautiful is typically studied and written about within the context of late-1800s and early-1900s American society's progression, it is often overlooked that City Beautiful planning transpired in Asia and Australasia. Consequently, considering the findings of these and other scholars is it now apt to think of the City Beautiful as an international city planning paradigm and not as an exclusively American urban design model?

The Element, in discussing the City Beautiful's application beyond the North American continent, is structured with numerous parts. The introductory section offers a summary of what the City Beautiful as an American planning model is. It presents important planning schemes composed at the end of the 1800s and during the early 1900s. In the opening section of the Element brief comment is also given with regard to Urban History's recent evolution.

In Sections 2, 3, 4, and 5 of the Element, case studies of City Beautiful planning in different countries are presented. Section 6 evaluates modern urban planning practice from a global historical perspective. The Element, all in all, spotlights how the City Beautiful was conceptualized in societies of disparate cultural, climatic, and political nature. Why the City Beautiful planning model was applied in those places is explained. Fundamentally, the Element informs of the growth of City Beautiful planning beyond the typical U.S.-centric historiographical standpoint. By doing this it adds to the knowledge of the history of urban planning's international propagation. Such wisdom matters because the physical imprint of the City Beautiful persists. The character of built fabrics in many parts of the world still shows the influence of the American urban design model.

From Section 2 onward, the Element recontextualizes international examples of City Beautiful planning. As I will show, the reach of the City Beautiful extends far beyond the U.S. territorial borders. Stelter (2000) and Freestone (2007a) have suggested that this diffusion was due to the growing popularity in different parts of the world of the need to have beautiful cities and the emergence of the modern city planning profession. However, did other factors have influence? Furthermore, if transnational urban historical inquiry emphasizes flows and movements of ideas, practices, and people, how did the process of configuring city environments in Asia, Australasia, and so on articulate the absorption of American ideas regarding urban environmental beauty? What made the City Beautiful approach so useful/relevant/important to the nations outside of North America?

To answer these questions, it is necessary to not only identify the physical forms taken by City Beautiful planning but also know what they mean. For example, what did the planning of urban environments denote of governance and its practice? Lawrence Vale (1992) and David Gordon (2018) reveal that authority and politics affect the need to present power and identity through the built fabric's form. Of relevance as well, how did modern planning information circulate? Comprehension of this is key to recognizing the City Beautiful's international imprint/success. Such knowledge will help unlock why it had the capacity to become a global planning phenomenon and assists too in enlightening why the urban past still informs urban designing in the present day.

1.1 The Emergence of City Beautiful Planning in the United States

For decades scholars have sought to understand how urban life was once lived and how towns and cities were once designed. Via investigating the relationship between the nature of society and the character of planning systems, they have collectively explained past human relations and the physical organization of urban communities. As a result, they have emphasized the need to know *who* practiced urban planning, *how* they designed urban places, and *what* urban environmental meanings existed in the setting of societal advancement.

Concerning city planning's evolution in the U.S. during the late 1800s and early-1900s, it was moulded by broadening comprehension of what 'good' housing, hygiene, and transportation systems were, *and* by growing knowledge of aesthetics and urban beautification. Central to this progress were American architects educated at the Ecole des Beaux Arts in Paris, France. Appraised by Madlen Simon (1996), Lauren O' Connell (2020), and Isabelle Gournay and Marie-Laurie Crosnier Leconte (2013), Ecole des Beaux Arts graduates against the backdrop of rapid national population growth and urbanization established new vocational schools, wrote regulations for architectural practice, and founded organizations in their homeland, such as The Society of Beaux-Arts Architects in 1894. Additionally, they composed 'progressive analyses'. Often published in the architectural press, these articles/discussions reinforced the perceived need for the expanding American nation to have 'good quality' edifices and environments for people to live and work in.

David Brain (1989) and Daniel T. Rodgers (1998) pinpoint 1893 as a watershed in the American process to improve urban environments. In that year the World's Columbian Exposition was held. Lasting from May to October, the event in Chicago became attributed with the birth of the planning movement known as 'City Beautiful' (Lamb, 1898). Central to its evolution was the Beaux Arts-educated architect-planner Daniel Burnham (1846–1912). He was enamoured by Paris's environmental design. The French capital's rebuilding in the mid-1800s by Georges Haussmann (1809–91) meant it transformed into a place that, in Burnham's view, 'has reached the highest state of development' (Burnham and Bennett, 1909: 14).

As a seminal event in the modern American planning narrative, the style, colour, and scale of the 1893 Chicago exposition's buildings, and their harmonious grouping by Burnham within a landscape designed by Frederick Law Olmsted (1822–1903), gave new public attention to urban design. The creation of the unified cityscape 'excited and impressed the thousands who came to Chicago and stepped into this environment, so novel to America' (Reps, 1965: 502). In particular, the Court of Honor (see Figure 1), with its monumental classical architectural grandeur and unity of effect (Schaffer, 2003), impressed visitors so much that it helped instil new social confidence in architects. In conjunction, it firmly established the Beaux Arts as *the* orthodoxy in American architecture and urban planning.

The American public's endorsement of grand urban design was bolstered by the 1901–2 *Improvement of the Park System of the District of Columbia*, that is, 'the first actual demonstration of the city beautiful movement's approach' (Stelter, 2000: 103). In revitalizing the U.S. capital city, its original environmental organization as designed in 1790 by Pierre L' Enfant (1754–1825) was fortified (Reps, 1983). By means of establishing monumental vistas between the Capitol, Washington Monument, and White House, Washington D.C.'s renewal generated a new interest in, and demand for, urban planning. Subsequently

Figure 1 The view westwards of the Court of Honor.
Source: Frederick Jackson (1895).

large-sized green spaces ('malls') and civic centre schemes were proposed in numerous towns and cities. Among the first large-sized settlements to implement such a feature was Cleveland, Ohio.

In discussing why urban planning became so important to the advancement of American society by the start of the twentieth century, Christine Boyer (1983) and Carl Smith (1994) isolate fear of social breakdown. At that time towns and cities were no longer seen by many members of society to yield any trace of wholesome community life; in fact, they symbolized disorder and danger. Consequently, an influential social-environmental belief was formed. It endorsed the perspective that well-designed urban places could uplift and educate the public in civic virtue. Crucially, a spatial model was identified. Situated at the heart of Washington D.C., the 1.5-mile-long, 300-foot-wide lawn known as The Mall was renewed as part of the *Improvement of the Park System of the District of Columbia*.

By about 1900 many well-off Americans deemed urban planning essential for the nation's future progress. Cleveland typified 'progressive "city sense"' (Rodgers, 1998: 170). With Daniel Burnham, John Carrére (1858–1911), and Arnold Brunner's (1857–1925) 1903 Group Plan facilitating the development of the lakefront, the laying out of new public spaces, and the construction of neo-classical edifices, the city to countless Americans embodied what modern urban design in the U.S. could accomplish. The visual quality of Cleveland's restructured built fabric was comparable, in the eyes of many, with the rebuilt cityscape of Paris by Haussmann (Howe, 1905).

The career of Daniel Burnham offers a rich written history. Still, as Robert Freestone stresses (2007a and 2023), it is imperative to recognize Burnham's vocational activities both inside and outside of the U.S., *and* to understand his influence upon foreign architects and planners. In fact, to wholly appreciate the internationalized nature of the City Beautiful two basic matters must be known. On the one hand, for any planning model to spread globally, processes must exist to export it overseas. On the other hand, processes must also exist for its importation into overseas societies. Stephen Ward (2002) in *Planning the Twentieth-Century City* clarifies this bilateral occurrence. In his view, imperial frameworks were central to the geographical spread of both the American City Beautiful and the British Garden City planning models. Mechanisms he identifies as being of importance to their global propagation include exhibitions, conferences, the publication of planning literature, the founding of international organizations, the holding of design competitions, and an international market demanding planning expertise and education.

Ward (2002) states that by 1900 the focus of American urban design thinking was the City Beautiful. According to William W. Wilson (1989: 1) it was a middle-/upper-middle-class effort to redesign cities 'into beautiful, functional entities'. Taking a holistic approach to urban planning, City Beautiful advocates sought to address the problems of American industrial settlements' rapid growth during the 1800s, for example, poverty, crime, poor sanitation, overcrowding, slum housing, ineffective and/or corrupt municipal governments (Morley, 2007), and tailor solutions to the alleged needs of the urban citizenry. Yet, as Anthony Sutcliffe (1981) and Robert Freestone (2023) discuss, whilst the City Beautiful Movement alluded to the concern of the whole urban community, it was informed by sectional motivations. When planning interventions were undertaken they often communicated messages aligned to power, authority, and patriotism. Then again, during the early 1900s the notion of utilizing comprehensive city planning to upgrade built fabrics metamorphosed into numerous real-world endeavours given that civic and business organizations commissioned urban plans. By and large, states Jon Peterson (2003), these schemes were composed by architects or landscape architects. They, as a result, acquired an elevated vocational status.

1.2 1893–1909: The Expansion of City Beautiful Planning in Practice

I earlier mentioned the importance of the World's Columbian Exposition and the revitalization of Washington, D.C. The renewal of the enormous green space in the heart of the U.S. capital city, The Mall (see Figure 2), instigated new unity between the settlement's buildings, open areas, and road layout (Moore, 1902). Pointedly, Chicago and Washington, D.C.'s urban planning model was European, not American. Indeed, regarding the capital's upgrading, Daniel Burnham along

Figure 2 An illustration showing the renewed Mall as proposed by *Improvement of the Park System of the District of Columbia*.

Source: The Plan for the National Capital, 9th Report of the Commission of Fine Arts (1923).

with Frederick Law Olmsted Jr. (1870–1957), Charles McKim (1847–1909), and Augustus St. Gaudens (1848–1907) spent five weeks in the summer of 1901 travelling to London, Paris, Rome, Venice, Vienna, Budapest, Frankfurt, and Berlin. Their purpose for touring Europe's 'great cities' was to examine past planning lessons and to realize how to bring them to the U.S. (Moore, 1902).

Charles Mulford Robinson, in *Modern Civic Art, or, The City Made Beautiful* (1904), explains that City Beautiful planning introduced new standards of environmental beauty, order, and dignity to American settlements. As the World's Columbian Exposition and improvement of Washington, D.C. explicitly demonstrate, urban beauty was to be instigated by clear-cut means: the design of individual, classical-styled public buildings; the laying out of symmetrical green spaces; and the orderly arrangement of buildings and spaces so that a relationship between them could be seen (Commission of Fine Arts, 1923; Moore, 1921a). In this framework civic centres acquired an idealized standing (Bennett, 1917); Cleveland's Group Plan is an exceptional example. Described in 1909 by the British author Inigo Triggs as producing magnificent visual results, the scheme inspired architects and civic organizations throughout the U.S. to

Figure 3 A photograph showing the southern end of the Mall in Cleveland. To the rear of the vista are the classically styled public library and courthouse.
Source: The author.

devise similar plans. What's more, urban beauty, manufactured from applying the architectural principles of proportion, harmony, balance, symmetry, and scale (Wilson, 1989), was believed by the twentieth century's commencement to articulate the authority of a local government (Robinson, 1901). To reside in a beautiful settlement verifies the conscientiousness of municipal officials.

Jon Peterson (2003) observes that during the twentieth century's first decade more than thirty-five American settlements were the subject of comprehensive City Beautiful plans, and, from 1910 to 1917, more than forty other places had major planning proposals. Among the most impressive, and well-known, are the plans for San Francisco and Chicago. Daniel Burnham composed the schemes. He, in San Francisco, reinvigorated the concept of monumental urban design; his 1905 plan (composed with Edward Bennett) sought to elevate the well-being of citizens (Draper, 1982; Kahn, 1979) by means of combining 'convenience and beauty in the greatest possible degree' (Burnham and Bennett, 1905: 35).

As the nucleus of the 'new city' (Haas, 2019), San Francisco's civic core was to have radial arteries running across it. However, with miles of waterfront and hillsides within the city's bounds, Burnham and Bennett's scheme organized streets, parkways, and boulevards so that they could correspond to the position of the shoreline and local hilltops. The result, states Herbert Croly, enables San Francisco's built fabric to 'become one of most precious national monuments of the American people' (1906: 436).

Burnham and Bennett's concept of unity between the built and natural environment was maintained in Chicago, where, in 1908, the *Plan for a Boulevard to Connect the North and South Sides of the River on Michigan Avenue and Pine Street* exposed their aspiration to restructure a large portion of the urban core. In fact, their appetite for exploiting planning for large-scale and long-term urban reform was most explicit in the 1909 *Plan for Chicago*. In this scheme they suggested the improvement of the lakefront, the establishment of highways within and beyond the city limits, and the creation of a city-wide park system (Mumford, 1961). Such environmental organization was to permit cultural advancement, economic growth, and more efficient civic administration to transpire (Burnham and Bennett, 1909).

Described by Patrick Abercrombie (1910: 56) as 'the most complete and sumptuous proposal for re-creating a town which has yet appeared in America', the *Plan of Chicago* was regarded by Carl Smith (2006: 86) as the product of 'thinking about Chicago and urban planning and also about how to present an alternate view of modern urban life as cogently as possible'. In summary, the 1909 scheme (Figure 4) made Burnham's name synonymous with the notion that urban planning must integrate ambitious societal advancement goals, or it will not stir the public's imagination (Hines, 2009).

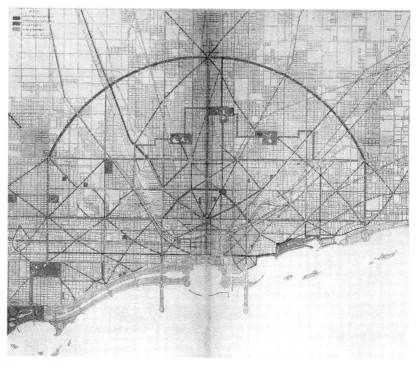

Figure 4 The 1909 plan of Chicago with street and boulevard, and park systems.
Source: Burnham and Bennett (1909).

2 The British City Beautiful

Explained in Section 1 of the Element, in the United States (U.S.) a new strategy for shaping urban environments materialized during the 1890s. Known as the City Beautiful, it proliferated throughout the country as the early-twentieth century unfolded. As will be discussed in Section 2 to Section 6 of the Element, City Beautiful planning had an international footprint. Accordingly, the ambition by the onset of the twentieth century to establish attractive, uplifting urban environments was not exclusive to the U.S. In Britain, for example, a City Beautiful phase transpired. Reaching its peak by the second decade of the twentieth century, the British focus on monumental artistic city planning offered an alternate approach to existent urban designing. So profound was the British admiration for artistic planning that it monopolized the contents of architecture publications and newly established planning journals, for example, *The Town Planning Review* (founded in 1910).

Central to the growth of the British City Beautiful was Aston Webb (1849–1930). Perhaps the most distinguished of all late-Victorian and

Edwardian architects, he in the role from 1902–4 of President of the Royal Institute of British Architects (RIBA) did much to cement the influence of the American City Beautiful upon British urban designing. Planning for monumental effect was, thanks to Webb, observable in London, for example the Queen Victoria Memorial Scheme (QVMS; see Figure 5), and in the provinces.

To comprehend how urban planning in Britain was affected by the American City Beautiful, it is necessary to recognize the disposition of British urbanism during the late 1800s and early 1900s, and to assess its changing character through the lens of Global Urban History. The inquiries of Kristin Stapleton (2022a), Gilbert A. Stelter (2000), and Daniel T. Rodgers (1998), therefore, must not be downplayed; they disclose that multi-directional flows of influence were able to shape how urban environments were designed by 1900.

Observes C.M. Allan (1965), foreign influence on the planning of British urban environments was apparent by as early as the late 1860s. From that time Scottish local governments expanded law to renovate whole urban districts 'on a modern basis', that is, along the lines of Haussmann's rebuilding of Paris. By the mid-1870s, English municipalities began to follow this example. Large-sized cities, including Birmingham and London, adopted slum clearing and the replanning of downtown sites with new boulevards as part of local governance. In London slum clearance continued into the early 1900s thanks to projects such as Kingsway-Aldwych. It, said Dirk Schubert and Anthony Sutcliffe (1996), was inspired by both Haussmann and Aston Webb's QVMS.

Stelter (2000: 101) remarks that by the early 1900s Haussmann's renovation of Paris 'had become the most emulated method of urban renewal in the world'. Rodgers (1998: 168), in dissecting the international influence of the French capital, suggests that, given the numerous activities Haussmann undertook, it is unsurprising that different nations in North America and Western Europe borrowed different strands of his work. Derivatives of the Paris rebuilding programme were formed in different places, he asserts, because of local elites' contrasting needs. In 1860s Berlin, Germany, political leaders embraced the Paris model given their interest in design monumentalism; in Britain, Paris was of influence to City Fathers owing to the necessity to improve sanitation and eliminate decrepit housing; and, by the late 1880s in the U.S., Haussmann's influence was apparent given the requirement to embellish/upgrade urban settings. Kristin Stapleton (2022a), with Rodger's conclusions in mind, draws attention to the matter of what constitutes a modern settlement. She reveals that the conception of an urban place as 'modern' is informed by official urban design models. So, how did the American City Beautiful become a model to the British?

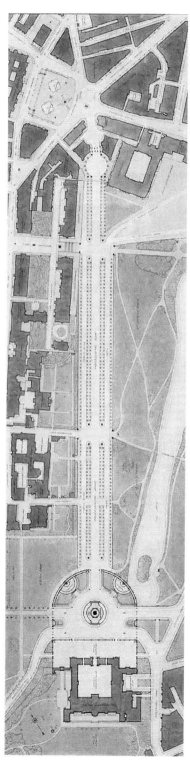

Figure 5 The winning plan by Aston Webb for the Queen Victorian Memorial Competition, published in *Illustrated London News*, 2 November 1901.

To answer the question it is necessary, state British planning history pioneers Gordon Cherry (1974) and Anthony Sutcliffe (1981), to understand shifting dynamics within society *and* the changing attitude of architects. Cherry notes that by the 1890s the philistinism of the Industrial Revolution bit deep into British artistic circles. Many architects no longer tolerated the visual disorder of town and cities. New urban design approaches were sought.

Building upon Cherry's viewpoint, the American influence is explained by Anthony Sutcliffe (1981) in relation to the British viewing a foreign urban design model as embodying both practical and aesthetic elements. He reasons that the concepts and practices aligned to the City Beautiful were easily comprehensible to the British because the American exemplar, first, carried forward modern planning practices known in Britain, for example, Haussmann's Paris, and, second, it expressed ideologies popularized earlier by well-known British artist-writers, for example, William Morris (1834–1896) and John Ruskin (1819–1900), that is, that art should be for all, not a few. The British City Beautiful was, by the second decade of the twentieth century, to bear its greatest fruit in four settlements. They form the focus of the next part of the Element.

2.1 The Rise of Monumental Planning in Britain: London, Cardiff, Bolton, and Dundee

To comprehend the nature of the British City Beautiful, Bolton, Cardiff, Dundee, and London must be referenced; they are the sites where the grandest examples of artistic planning occurred. However, their plans also reveal the political, cultural, and economic motives as to why the British embraced American-style planning projects. To this end, and citing Stelter (2000), he remarks that artistic planning became an international matter by the start of the twentieth century due to three fundamentals: because of the emergence of the notion in planning circles that a city can be viewed as a piece of art; because of changing leadership within national planning communities; and, owing to evolving urban theory. It emphasized the value of holistic rather than piecemeal urban designing to the process of environmental improvement.

Aston Webb, as indicated before, had an enormous reputation in British architectural circles. He held enormous weight when planning was formalized into law with legislation such as the 1909 Housing, Town Planning, Etc. Act. His stardom was confirmed in 1901 by overseeing the QVMC's design, and in 1902 by the RIBA presidency. His role as RIBA President, and afterwards as the chairman of the RIBA's Town Planning Committee, helped direct the advancement of British planning. Webb acknowledged, for instance, the social value of civic art and at the RIBA's 1910 Town Planning Conference, the first major event of its kind in the world, he asserted an unlimited opportunity existed for artistic urban designing. Of note too, he had high-level American contacts. In 1903, Webb awarded the RIBA's highest award, the Royal Gold Medal, to the American architect Charles McKim (1847–1909). By 1907, Webb was awarded the American Institute of Architects' Gold Medal. As an agent uniting British and American urban design through planning practice and dialogue, in 1916 he built upon the success of the QVMS and composed the Charing Cross Improvement Scheme (CCIS).

To identify the origin of the American City Beautiful's influence upon British urban planning, one strong possibility is a 1900 speech given by Webb to the Architectural Association. In the presentation Webb speaks of architecture requiring a 'fourth dimension', namely that buildings must be placed into a fitting environment. Reinforcing this standpoint in a 1903 speech, the now-RIBA president called upon architects, civil engineers, and surveyors to work together so that British planning could be 'properly shaped'. Specifically, in calling out the perceived unartistic form of the British built fabric, Webb (1903: 8) implored architects to consider urban planning as an important vocational endeavour. Without this, 'city usefuls' rather than 'city beautifuls' will be established, plus, 'a large part of the [urban design] work, which is already greatly encroached upon, would finally slip away from architects altogether'.

In 1903 Webb proposed the creation of an advisory body modelled on the U.S.' Council of Fine Arts. Such an organization, identified Triggs (1909), was to advise re urban improvement at the municipal and national levels. Besides, after inviting Charles McKim to London to receive the RIBA Gold Medal, it was noted that the American left two gifts at the Institute, a book on contemporary American architectural practice, and another book on the 1901–2 Washington, D.C. plan. Webb (1903: 8), speaking of this publication, said: 'I commend a study of this book to all interested – and what architect is not? – in the laying out and improvement of our great cities.' No doubt inspired by McKim's gift, Webb soon thereafter promoted the preservation of London's garden squares and with, Norman Shaw (1831–1912), he put forward a scheme to remodel Piccadilly Circus. On the importance of urban planning to societal development, Webb (1904: 431) said: 'practical men are beginning to realise that noble dispositions in a town, noble streets and buildings, are an education as necessary for the higher development of patriotism and public spirit as good water and sanitation are necessary for the bodily well-being.' However, from a practical standpoint, to grasp Webb's imprint upon the British City Beautiful's manifestation, it is necessary to know of the QVMS and CCIS.

The critical success of the QVMS, as emphasized by both the mainstream press and the architectural press, served as a catalyst for artistic planning ideas and practice in Britain. Initiated in 1901 to honour Queen Victoria (1819–1901), *and* to provide for a 'better' London as a national and imperial capital, the scheme with its laying out of the Mall roadway at the front of Buckingham Palace, the construction of Admiralty Arch, and the refacing of Buckingham Palace's east elevation, served to inspire British architects pertaining to improving the appearance and spatial organization of industrial towns and cities. Occurring at a time when urban environments were defined by visual chaos, the coherent character of Webb's plan with its large-sized classical buildings, enormous green spaces, statuary, and broad roadways, contrasted from the visual mess and the high densities of British urban settlements. Critically, the momentum for grand city planning established by the QVMS did not end in London upon the project's completion in 1912.

In 1916, with John Burns (1858–1943) and Reginald Blomfield (1856–1942), Webb composed the CCIS. It sought to bring improvements to inner city London by means of exploiting the capital's most important natural environmental feature, the River Thames. Viewed by the public as one of the most important improvement schemes in the city's lengthy history, the CCIS intended to alleviate traffic congestion and instigate far-reaching improvement in the civic architecture of London. The extensive nature of the planning scheme incorporated proposing the construction of a new bridge, a new road layout north and south of the Thames, Charing Cross Station being moved to the Thames' South Bank, and a new monumental roadway being laid out. This boulevard was to complement the development of the Kingsway-Aldwych and QVMS, and so form a major axis between St Martin's Church and St Martin's Place on the North Bank and, on the South Bank, Charing Cross Station's new location.

In Cardiff, at approximately the same time as London was undertaking the QVMS, the Cathays Park district of the settlement was developed; see Figure 6. As the premier City Beautiful civic centre in Britain, numerous public edifices were built on land hitherto owned by the 3rd Marquis of Bute (1847–1900). Articulating the aspiration of local elites for Cardiff to become the national capital of Wales, between 1897 and 1915 a new public edifice was constructed in Cathays Park about every two years.

To understand why an impressive civic centre was built in Cardiff, it is vital to know the settlement's industrial and demographic expansion during the nineteenth century. The first census of England and Wales, in 1801, recorded Cardiff's population as a little over 1,800; by 1901, it was approximately eighty times larger. By that time, as Britain's preeminent coal-exporting port, Cardiff's enlargement instigated much civic pride. In promoting Cardiff as the embryonic metropolis of modern Wales – it being given city status in 1905, the local elites' desire to establish a cityscape dissimilar to anything else in the country was

Figure 6 An aerial view of Cathays Park in 1933.

Source: The Royal Commission on the Ancient and Historical Monuments of Wales (license 001246/1).

paramount (Morley, 2009). Explains P.J. Waller (1983), Cardiff's urban design was to reveal and feed civic self-esteem.

The transformation of Cathays Park from a 57-acre green space to a City Beautiful-type environment is a remarkable if unappreciated story of British planning history. Said by J.B. Hilling (1976) and J.M. Freeman (1990) to be more than a mere exercise in designing large-sized buildings, the establishment of an imposing civic centre was about providing an administrative and cultural hub not just for Cardiff, but *for Wales*. The result was 'unquestionably the finest example of forethought, enterprise and the grasp of the underlying principles which make for civic art.' (Mawson, 1911: 42).

To appreciate the application of contemporary American concepts of urban design in Cathays Park, I stress certain matters must be given attention. First, as I touch upon previously in the Element, by about 1900 many British architects saw opportunity to create more functional *and* beautiful urban environments. Second, to accomplish this necessitated a search overseas for inspiration. Third, with reference to the designers of the edifices in Cathays Park – Henry Lanchester (1863–1953), Edwin Rickard (1872–1920), James Stewart (1865–1908), W.D. Caröe (1857–1938) Arnold Dunbar Smith (1866–1933), and Percy Thomas (1883–1969), they collectively sought to establish a sense of association between their buildings, that is, enact a long-established ideal of civic art (Adshead, 1910). The total effect of this strategy was to amplify the visual impression of the district (Morley, 2009).

In the frame of British planning's development, the importance of grand plans for the provincial industrial settlements of Bolton and Dundee should not be disregarded. Whilst in London and Cardiff, City Beautiful designing was

Figure 7 James Thompson's proposed plan for Dundee, with railway station
and civic centre in the background.

Source: *The Town Planning Review* (1913).

employed to establish an 'appropriate' face to settlements of, or aspiring to be,
national capitals, with regard to Dundee and Bolton the promotion of civic pride
and the patronage of art were fundamentals in the adoption of large-scale urban
planning. In Dundee the city architect, James Thompson (1852–1927), put
forward a comprehensive to renew the downtown and waterfront (Figure 7).
The Town Planning Review remarked that the scheme intended to 'provide
Dundee with the most magnificent river front in Great Britain' (1913: 177).

Analogous to Cardiff, Dundee had grown rapidly during the 1800s. *The Builder*
said of the city: 'Considering the age, the historic importance and the present
size and wealth of Dundee, it is disappointingly wanting in architectural interest'
(1898: 139). In renewing a seventy-plus-acre area of the urban core, Thompson's
plan involved reclaiming land from the Tay Estuary, slum removal, bridge building, public edifice construction, and establishment of gardens and tree-lined
avenues. In expanding the local practice of planning beyond slum clearing and
road building, Thompson's project represented a new direction in Dundee's
environmental management and design. For his effort to assist a municipality
not overflowing with spare funds but strongly desiring to effect urban improvement, he was lauded in journals such as *The Builder* (1915a) and *The Town
Planning Review* (1913). Thompson was the hero of British urban renewal.

Thompson's scheme anchored itself to establishing a large, symmetrically-
formed open area described as a pleasure ground and esplanade (The Builder,
1915a: 585). The most prominent of the new civic edifices, the classical-style

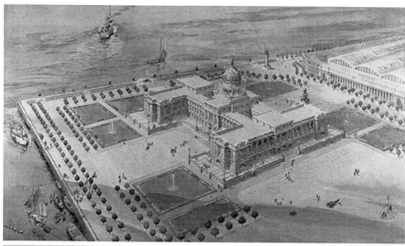

Figure 8 Perspectives of the Municipal Office, Dundee.
Source: *The Town Planning Review* (1913).

Municipal Office, was to have its visual presence enhanced by a huge dome positioned at the centre of its rooftop. Statues were to be placed about the building's site. A fundamental element of Thompson's plan was, as I mention before, land reclamation. Similar to the Pier Head scheme in Liverpool, a vast tract of land from the local estuary was retrieved. This new land was to bestow Dundee 'a splendid site for its new municipal building and public market, and a fine open space on the river front.' (The Town Planning Review, 1913: 177).

   The Builder (1915b: 31) stated that Thompson's scheme 'although appearing somewhat ambitious at first sight, is both practicable and economic in its adaptation of means to ends'. The journal added that it 'is also so arranged that it can be carried out in sections, none of them of great size or cost, which can be put in hand at intervals of a long period of time, avoiding a heavy charge of rates'. Unfortunately, Thomson's project, in keeping with so many urban improvement schemes put forward during the early years of King George V's reign (1910–36), was subsequently abandoned. With the commencement of World War One in 1914 it and countless other urban design enterprises were halted. Nevertheless, if Dundee had developed along the lines originally proposed by Thompson in 1913, then it would have acquired an urban core on a par with numerous large-sized cities in the U.S. (Figure 8).

In 1914, Stanley Adshead insisted that for artistic British planning to be a success, it had to possess capacity to rouse people's interest in the urban environments where they live and work. Recalling Daniel Burnham's dictum that planning must 'stir men's blood' (Burnham and Bennett, 1909), Adshead stated that great cities are characterized by wide streets, large buildings, expansive open spaces, *and* dignity and order (1914: 188). To accomplish this in Britain, he asserted that planners must understand past planning traditions and recognize that 'the highest conception of a city is an aggregation of human dwellings adorned with associations' (Adshead, 1914: 188). Accordingly, planners need to ensure 'the convenience of the community, but also be dictator of the arts, leader of fashion in building, and arbiter in matters pertaining to architectural character and style' (1914: 189). Significantly, such rationalism was already evident in Bolton. In 1910 Thomas Mawson (1861–1933), sponsored by wealthy local industrialist William Lever (1851–1925), presented the *Proposed Improvement Scheme for the Borough of Bolton*. It was to 'transform the town into the "city beautiful"' (Mawson, 1911: 273; see Figure 9).

To reform Bolton's appearance, and to reorganize its layout, Mawson focused upon three downtown environmental features: the Town Hall and Town Hall Square; the Parish Church; and, Queen's Park. Within the town's principal green open area, Mawson recommended a new Art Gallery and Museum to be built and a causeway marked by statuary to be laid out east-west through the park's grounds. With its entrances adorned by impressive pylons, the new promenade space was to provide not only direct access from Bolton's western suburbs to the urban core; along the walkway citizens were to be afforded impressive views of the local built environment. The Art Gallery and Museum, to have maximum impact upon the onlooking eye, was to sit on the crown of the hill within Queen's Park. It 'would form the most prominent landmark for miles round' (Mawson, 1911: 271).

At the front of the Art Gallery and Museum Mawson (1911) proposed a curved entranceway. It was to lead to the Art Gallery and Museum's forecourt and main entrance. Coupled with the magnificent sweeping curve that led from Queen's Park to the Town Hall, the new boulevard was to provide both a traffic route and

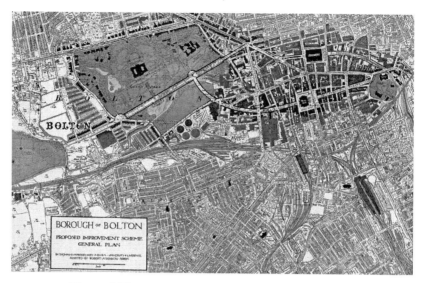

Figure 9 Thomas Mawson's proposed plan for Bolton.
Source: Mawson (1911).

a processional way (Mawson, 1911). Comparable to James Thompson's planning proposal for Dundee, Mawson's approach to monumental urban designing in Bolton sought to unify the townscape and enhance the local sense of place. By utilizing the uniqueness of Bolton's undulating site, the 1910 plan intended to promote beauty in civic life, ease traffic congestion, centralize municipal activities, and stimulate economic and cultural growth. Civic pride was to consequently swell, and the town's new environmental form was to set an example for every urban place in Britain to follow. From a planning perspective, Bolton was to 'fire the imagination and raise the ideal' (Mawson, 1911: 273).

2.2 Liverpool University, the RIBA's London Conference, and International Planning Exchange

Within Section 2 of the Element a handful of individuals are documented as being instrumental to City Beautiful planning practice in Britain. If seeking to know more of the British adoption of City Beautiful designing, then it is vital to recognize the role of the urban planning media, the holding of international conferences, and the founding of new planning schools and institutes.

In 1909, at the University of Liverpool, the Department of Civic Design was opened. Not only did the Department quickly garner much attention given its status as Britain's only planning school, its reputation was also greatly enhanced one year later by the launch of world's first English language planning journal,

The Town Planning Review. Publishing papers on the evolution of planning in Britain, Australia, continental Europe, and the U.S., many of the Department's staff contributed articles, for example, Patrick Abercrombie (1879–1957), Stanley Adshead (1868–1946), Charles Reilly (1878–1948), and Thomas Mawson. Other staff at the Department of Civic Design included John Brodie (1858–1934). He was a civil engineer employed by Liverpool's municipal government, and he was responsible for applying American planning techniques so that a city-wide system of roads linked to parks could be established.

Considering *The Town Planning Review*'s rapidly earned repute, Ward (2002) identified that soon after its founding additional publications, for example, *Papers and Discussions* and *Journal of the Town Planning Institute*, were launched. Alongside the setting up of other planning schools, for example, at University College London in 1914, these new journals expanded British interest in urban planning and consolidated the enthusiasm established by events such as the 1907 City Beautiful Conference in Liverpool and the October 1910 RIBA Town Planning Conference in London. In exposing British students and design practitioners to foreign planning activities, the media reinforced the international dimension within British planning. So too did the published Transactions of the RIBA's conference. In the opinion of Thomas Adams (1936), it is an indispensable document for British architects and planners.

With delegates from Australia, Belgium, Canada, France, Germany, Holland, Ireland, Italy, Spain, Sweden, Switzerland, and North America, the RIBA's convention was a site of transnational intellectual exchange with star practitioners/theorists/speakers that included Daniel Burnham; the subsequent publication of the conference's Transactions allowed for all presentations to be chronicled and, so, disseminated worldwide. At the RIBA's conference, and representing the American planning community, Burnham referenced the fact that modern urban designing in the U.S. of 'the present movement is very short; it goes back less than ten years' (Burnham, 1911a: 106). The London event, he said, therefore affords 'the opportunity to meet and see the best work of others' (Burnham, 1911a: 107). With this in mind, and to enable the 1,200-plus conference attendees to gain supplementary knowledge of American planning, the RIBA ensured space was provided for an exhibit on contemporary schemes in the U.S. (Art and Progress, 1910: 206).

At the RIBA's conference, Burnham gave a presentation titled 'A City of the Future under a Democratic Government'. In the speech he referenced the connection between the needs of citizens and the character of urban plans. Declaring that in democratic society laws must be made fit for purpose, for Burnham planning law should be applied to establish environmental features such as neighbourhood parks. They, he said, 'are the promoters of sanity, and in city planning they should be placed before everything else, and they will, in another generation, return ample dividends in the shape of happy, self-controlled men and women' (1911b: 378). He concluded that whilst the character of the built environment does not change an individual's personality, 'it does modify him for good and evil'. In review, Whyte (2012) identified that the 1910 conference underscored two rudiments in national planning movements at that time: the importance of domestic agendas, and the existence of transnational networks. Furthermore, against the backdrop of rising interest in, and new publications of urban planning, Cherry (1974) points out the need to not disregard the significance of the founding of the Town Planning Institute in 1914. It, among other things, helped to reiterate the social purpose of British urban planning and was an influential agent upon centralizing planning education *and* the shaping of government policy re urban environmental management during and after the end of World War One.

Anthony Sutcliffe (1981: 173) detects that by the time of World War One's occurrence, some planners in Britain were alluding to the existence of an international planning movement. To assess if their understanding is correct, he notes the need to recognize whether truly international planning tendencies overrode national ones. In undertaking such assessment four matters must be considered. First, the different types of planners that existed during the early 1900s: 'the fully cosmopolitan planner; the intermediary; the home-based planner with the willingness to look abroad; and, the xenophobe' (1981: 173). Second, that national planning movements comprised collections of persons with varying levels of international awareness. The cosmopolitan planners 'were few in number but highly influential' (1981: 173). Third, these pluralistic-minded professionals actually diverged in their evaluation of what modern planning is. Some judged it to be an art, while others viewed it as a science. Consequently, four, whilst they had great sway within national planning movements, typically they each 'pursued a different course' (Sutcliffe, 1981: 175). In other words, they imported/applied contemporary American planning notions and practices to different degrees.

For Sutcliffe, knowledge of conceptual factors deepens comprehension of why a planning model can internationally diffuse. He acknowledges, for instance, that early-1900s planning *was* subject to the effect of artistic influence but, with regard to the political-legal instruments of planning within different nations, though initially developed in reaction to national or even local circumstances they were 'liable to adoption elsewhere through the processes of *innovation diffusion*' (1981: 180). Moreover, even though the world of the early 1900s was defined by competing nation states, conditions within countries helped to *persuade* individuals 'to make decisions which they might not have made in response to national conditions alone' (1981: 180). Yet, he reflects, distinguishing these three matters through examining professionals and their activities is not straightforward. They are 'rarely aware of such clear divisions' (Sutcliffe, 1981: 188). Plus, planning as an international phenomenon during the early 1900s was 'too pervasive, too confusing'. Even now, as scholars from different disciplines venture to explain the propagation of historical planning models between countries at the start of the twentieth century, evidence shows that local, regional, national, international, and personal factors intermixed.

2.3 The British Imperial City Beautiful

To conclude Section 2 of the Element, notice is given to the exportation of British urban planning practice via imperial channels.

In early-1900s Canada, the City Beautiful took hold from three roots: Canadian designers looking to the U.S. for examples of reintroducing order and beauty into their cities (Stelter, 2000); the establishment of U.S.-style municipal organizations, and planning schemes composed by Americans; and planning projects composed by British designers, for example, Robert Mattocks, and Thomas Mawson – for Banff, Calgary, Regina, and Vancouver. Mattocks graduated from the Department of Civic Design at the University of Liverpool, and in 1915 was awarded first prize in the Vancouver Civic Center design competition. Mawson, a lecturer at the aforesaid planning school, designed the 1914 plan for Calgary. Arguably, alongside the Calgary Plan, the peak of City Beautiful influence was the *Report of the Federal Plan Commission on a General Plan for the Cities of Ottawa and Hull*. It was composed in 1915 by the Beaux Arts-trained Edward Bennett, a foremost City Beautiful proponent and professional partner of Daniel Burnham. Among the features put forward for Ottawa's environmental improvement was a new civic district filled with neo-classical buildings in proximity to the shoreline of the Ottawa River. For Bennett, as he remarks in John Nolen's edited volume *City Planning* (1917), well-designed and conveniently sited public edifices and public spaces distinguish a city.

During the first decade of the twentieth century City Beautiful influence upon Canadian urbanism was evident in the form of American municipal-type documents such as the one composed by the Toronto Guild of Civic Art. Its *Report on a Comprehensive Plan for Systematic Civic Improvements in Toronto* (1909) summarized the role of planning in order to accomplish the city's improvement/beautification; in facilitating both social and environmental betterment the local road pattern was to be reshaped. The notion of civic improvement and the practice of city planning, the Report noted, 'are the remedies for the evils of the congestion of population in cities' (Toronto Guild of Art, 1909: 3).

local nature of life but the form and meaning of the colonial built fabric too. Central to the early establishment of the American colonial urban design narrative was Daniel Burnham, who in 1904–5 visited the country and through his 1905 plan for Manila and his 1905 scheme for Baguio, offered a new paradigm to reshape the appearance and plan of Philippine settlements. Critical to Burnham's influence was the need to green towns and cities, and his City Beautiful influence was to last until the early 1940s thanks to the activities of Filipinos employed by the Bureau of Public Works (BPW).

In coming to terms with Burnham's impact, one must pay attention to his 7,000-word *Report on Proposed Improvements at Manila*. Published in June 1905 with co-author Pierce Anderson (1870–1924), the document outlines the environmental transitions to occur as part of the American agenda to modernize the capital city and thereby 'uplift' and 'civilize' Filipinos in accord with President William McKinley's Benevolent Assimilation Proclamation (issued on 21 December 1898). The declaration, to be brief, described Americans 'not as invaders or conquerors, but as friends, to protect the natives' (Miller, 1984: 25). As part of this 'security', the Americans were to transform the natives into 'our little brown brothers' (Wolff, 1961).

The importation of American civilization to Southeast Asia was hoped to catalyse a new level of societal advancement. As I have explained in *Cities and Nationhood: American Imperialism and Urban Design in the Philippines, 1898–1916* (2018a), American colonial governance in the Philippine Islands was anchored in certain fundamentals: economic progress; political reform; advancement of public education and public health; infrastructure development; and, city planning. In some regards, alteration of the built environment post-1898 was necessary. Manila, for instance, had a reputation for unsanitary living conditions and infectious illness. Life expectancy was much lower than that of towns and cities in North America (Morley, 2021). Also, many of Manila's roads were impassable during the wet season (Torres, 2010). William D. Boyce, writing in 1914, summarized Manila's environmental conversion post-1905. He remarked, 'the unsanitary, dreamy city of old' had been transformed into a clean, healthful, up-to-date capital; 'It is the head and heart of a nation we hope to "Manila-ize" throughout' (1914: 30).

In the *Report on Proposed Improvements at Manila*, Burnham and Anderson (1906: 635) outline what Manila of the future was to be. As a city that was to 'become the adequate expression of the destiny of the Filipino people as well as an enduring witness to the efficient services of America in the Philippine Islands', Burnham and Anderson proposed a number of environmental transitions. These included a road system comprising of a 250-feet-wide, seven-mile-long 'Sea Boulevard' along the Manila Bay shoreline so to link Manila with the port settlement of Cavite (see Figure 11); circumferential parkways at the urban fringe; diagonal arteries to link districts together north and south of the Pasig River; and 930 symmetrically formed blocks of land orientated to enable buildings to face towards direct sunlight during particular times of the day. Drawing

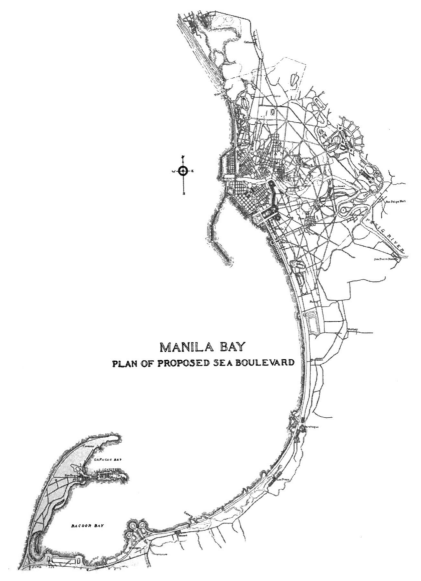

MANILA BAY
PLAN OF PROPOSED SEA BOULEVARD

Figure 11 Burnham and Anderson's 1905 plan for Manila with Sea Boulevard connecting the capital city to the port of Cavite.

Source: Burnham and Anderson (1906).

inspiration from Washington, D.C., Manila's new street pattern was to provide more liberated movement about the city than had ever existed (Morley, 2018a). With new roads to be lined by trees and grass banks, 'New Manila' was to promote contemporary standards of beauty and offer a cityscape entirely distinct from what had existed pre-1898.

In contrast from the urban form developed by Spain's Laws of the Indies (1573), the American planners' recommendation to lay out long, straight, and broad thoroughfares lined with landscape architecture features (Kirsch, 2017) was to supply new visual coherence to a settlement originally formed with separate residential quarters for the European, Chinese, Japanese, and native populations. Inspiration for Manila's restructuring came from Europe. Utilizing the model of French park systems, Burnham and Anderson intended citizens to undertake urban journeys without losing sight at any time of green foliage (Morley, 2018a). Taking the example too of the work implemented by the South Park Board in Chicago, playing fields were to be scattered throughout the Philippine capital and, at the urban periphery, several large-sized parks laid out. At the urban core, in proximity to where the American planners recommended the building of a new civic core, was to be founded a pair of large parks. Today known as Rizal Park and Burnham Green (see Figure 12) the open spaces were to encourage social bonding and moral improvement (Morley, 2018a). In generating civic spirit and pride, people, irrespective of their racial heritage, social class, age, gender, life experiences, and so on, could *come together in open areas as Manileños.*

Whilst during the Spanish colonial era the physical, cultural, and political heart of Manila had been the fortified settlement known as *Intramuros* ('within the walls'), by 1905 its moat had been backfilled and turned into a lawn (Morley, 2021). The nucleus of 'Modern Manila' was put into the area of the city known as *Extramuros* ('outside the walls'). The symbolism of this environmental shift was great; no more was *Intramuros* the physical and allegorical heart of Manila and the Philippines. Now, in *Extramuros* was to be the civic centre labelled by Burnham and Anderson as the 'Government Group'. Containing the Capitol and a large-sized building to house various government departments, nearby was to be sited the Hall of Justice, Library, Museum, Exposition Building and, at the southern bank of the Pasig River, the Post Office. With its symmetrical layout the Government Group possessed a visual dignity previously unseen in Manila. In transforming Manila into, literally, a 'Pearl of the Orient', practical matters were not neglected. The clustering of different offices was also to aid the efficient work of the colonial government.

Figure 12 A view in late 2023 westwards across Roxas Boulevard towards
Rizal Park and the Rizal Monument.

Source: The author.

Manila's transformation under the auspices of Burnham's and Anderson's
prowess was to arise not only from the grand neo-classical facades of Manila's
new public edifices but also from the careful organizing of its new public
edifices in relation to each other. A grand planning axis, inspired by the
historical examples of Rome, Italy, and Versailles, France, was to anchor the
layout of the Government Group. Traversing east–west through the civic core,
the axis was to be marked by monuments, for example the Rizal Monument
(erected 1913), the principal entrance of the Capitol, and the building's large
dome. Significantly, too, the planning alignment was to extend out from the
civic district. To the east of the Capitol's east-facing elevation were to be axes
radiating along broad, lengthy thoroughfares to the suburbs and, in the case of
the avenue heading towards the district of Paco, to the city's new train station.
To the west of the Capitol, the central planning axis of the Government Group
was to traverse through the spaces now known as Rizal Park and Burnham
Green to the shoreline where 'a special pier with enlarged approaches and
suitable accessories will lend itself to treatment in accord with this function as
the principal water gate of Manila' (Burnham and Anderson, 1906: 633).

The natural environment, particularly water features, were exploited by
Burnham and Anderson (1906: 635) given that they saw opportunity with
their plan 'to create a unified city equal to the greatest of the western world,

with unparalleled and priceless addition of a tropical setting'. Manila Bay was judged by the planners as analogous to the Bay of Naples in Italy, and the winding Pasig River as Manila's equivalent of the River Seine in Paris. Numerous *esteros* (estuarine inlets) were to be revitalized as part of the 1905 city plan. Burnham and Anderson perceived their aesthetic worth as similar to the canals of Venice, Italy. In the fullest sense, Manila's redevelopment was to physically and symbolically distance it from the era of Spanish colonial rule, and all that it entailed. Truly, the 1905 city plan was to demonstrate that a new civilization in the Philippine Islands had begun.

Burnham's and Anderson's use of monumental planning axes was not limited to Manila. At Baguio, in taking up the British concept of the hill station developed in 1800s India (Crossette, 1999; Reed, 1976), they proposed the transformation of a barren, upland site into a single, unified built environment. Akin to Manila, Baguio was to act as a medium for the U.S. colonial message, and the layout of the city was to integrate natural environmental features (Vernon, 2010a).

Designed not to exceed 25,000 residents, Baguio, sited in the Benguet Highlands at about 5,000 feet above sea level, was to offer respite from the oppressive summer heat and humidity of Manila in the Central Luzon lowlands. At the core of the new city, in the mile-long valley (Moore, 1921b) known locally as *kafagway*, Burnham and Anderson in 1905 envisaged an esplanade. It marked the main axis of the urban plan although, following William E. Parsons's employment as consulting architect, the original plan was amended (Rebori, 1917a); a large park was now placed on the primary planning alignment (see Figure 13). Subsequently named Burnham Park, the principal planning axis of Baguio was to have its ends marked by the National Government Buildings and the City Hall.

The generic impression of Baguio from the outset was that it sat *within* the distinct upland landscape (Vernon, 2020). Put simply, the new city was to have a cityscape unique to the Philippine Islands. The road system originally put forward by Burnham, and maintained by Parsons, utilized local topography. Its form reinforced the city plan's sense of place. For example, roads ran to/from commanding locales such as the peaks of pine-tree covered hills. This road configuration was said to have been inspired by Burnham's knowledge of Italian, French, and Japanese hilltop settlements (Morley, 2018a). In contrast, the downtown layout bore much resemblance to City Beautiful projects in the U.S. With Parsons having been educated at Columbia University and Yale University, he was, like many of his American contemporaries, greatly knowledgeable of the Beaux Arts.

By modifying Burnham and Anderson's original scheme (which was drawn up after a few days' visit to Baguio – see Moore, 1921a), Parsons was able to

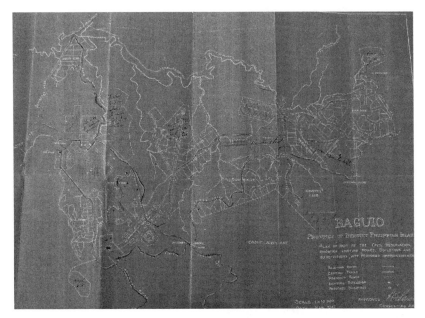

Figure 13 The March 1907 city plan for Baguio by William E. Parsons, that is, the first planning scheme to suggest a grand park at the urban core.
Source: NND760024, 350–150–56–15–2 U.S. National Archives II.

reinforce the grand axis formed between the National Government Buildings and City Hall and, in consequence, he bolstered the visual relationship between the national and local government edifices. As I argue (Morley, 2018a), the two most conspicuous edifices in Baguio, the municipal and national government offices, looked directly towards each other; this symbolized the 'practical political education' promoted by the Americans post-1898. Such allegory within the city plan was not accidental. Baguio prior to the American colonial imprint in the Benguet Highlands was renowned for tribalism. Now, with Burnham's city plan in hand, the American colonial government could build public offices; educate the local population about law, civil liberties, and democratic politics; and transform a rural hinterland until then inhabited by Igorot tribespeople into a beautiful city in which people could live and work in 'modern fashion'.

The transformation of Baguio into a modern city that was the economic and political hub of its upland region, articulates the capacity of the American colonial regime to 'liberate', 'uplift', and 'civilize' (Tinio McKenna, 2017; see Figure 14). Paul Kramer (2006: 191) labels this evolution as 'calibrated colonialism'. He remarks that it entails 'progress' by means of the colonized

Figure 14 Top: Baguio's site in 1901, and (bottom) the same view twenty five years later.

Source: American Historical Collection, Rizal Library, Ateneo de Manila University.

population attaining American-set behavioural markers. In turn, this exposes the Filipinos' potential to responsibly exercise power in the future. Vital to the socialization process in Baguio was the bringing together of Americans and Filipinos and, in Parsons' revised plan, this was to occur within the centrally located green space known as Burnham Park. Popular with residents and tourists, Burnham Park since the early 1900s has been the primary open area in Baguio. Its popular use in past times articulates the success of the City Beautiful blueprint for the organization of space, but the importance of the green space in the present day is expressed by heritage advocates. They recognize that their city is the only large-sized provincial capital in the Philippines with a monumental downtown park. Even with its colonial origins and association with the imposition of American power and control, the central space is viewed as a green asset given the context of Baguio's ever-expanding and ever-densifying built fabric.

3.2 The City Beautiful in the Philippine Provinces

Between 1905 and 1919 city planning in the Philippines was undertaken by Americans employed as 'consulting architect' by the colonial government, specifically William E. Parsons, George Fenhagen, and Ralph H. Doane. The individual initially key to the transmission of Burnham's City Beautiful planning model beyond Manila and Baguio was Parsons. As a case in point, in Zamboanga on the largely Muslim-populated Mindanao Island, he composed a monumental city plan. With a new civic centre, and with tree-lined roadways up to one-hundred feet wide, Zamboanga's new Capitol Building was to be surrounded by public spaces and situated close to the shoreline so to be visible to passing ships. In carrying forward Burnham's striking models of Manila and Baguio, Parsons consolidated the design of space and roads evident in the capital city and summer colonial capital as part of societal reform in the south of the Philippine Archipelago.

To generalize, prior to 1898 Philippine urban settlements were characterized by grid plans with centrally-located, church-lined plazas (*plaza majors*). But, by the early 1900s new public buildings and spaces, located downtown or at the urban fringe, showcased the establishment of civic society and a new governmental system. In articulating liberation from Spanish colonial rule, and its association (in American eyes) with 'backwardness', to the Americans new architecture, spaces, and monuments played a vital role in informing Filipinos of the basics of their evolving nation. It also envisioned their country as a unified territory with a democratic government and united citizenry, that is, a body politic encompassing *all Filipinos*, not just a Christian population in certain parts of the island chain. Philippine built fabrics, as a result, were by the 1900s not only to look different but to assume different cultural and political meaning than before. By showcasing modernity, the largest settlements were to have classically-styled architecture, wide roads, parks, trains and electric trams, clean water systems, modern sewers, and industrial technologies that encouraged economic growth: 'The 'modern Philippine city' (as based on Daniel Burnham's City Beautiful paradigm) became a fundamental ploy, along with schools and political training and the like, to building a new level of civilization' (Morley, 2018a: 143). Without societal advancement, affirms Adas (2014), the Americans believed the Filipinos could not be readied for future self-rule.

In Zamboanga, Parsons' planning scheme with its new buildings, roads, and public spaces 'was also about permitting the American colonial regime to extend the 'national community' to a geographical and cultural territory formerly outside the confines of colonial rule' (Morley, 2018a: 144). Likewise, in Cebu, his 1912 city plan (Figure 15) conformed to Burnham's concept of making modern-era settlements 'convenient for commerce and attractive and healthful as a place of residence' (Parsons, 1915: 13). Once again, a new civic core and boulevards radiating to/from it were on display; 'these two features became a basic component of the 'modern Philippine city' by 1916' (Morley, 2018a: 122).

The Cebu city plan comprised a handful of core environmental features: a seafront boulevard/redeveloped shoreline; a new civic district, monumental boulevards from the downtown business district; and, the integration of Spanish colonial architectural elements. As was the case with Burnham in Manila, Parsons's Cebu scheme integrated the Spanish fort and *plaza mayor*, albeit with a greatly diminished environmental role. Whereas before 1898 they symbolized Spanish power, in the 1912 planning scheme they were to serve as leisure sites for the public. In fact, in Cebu, by shifting the built fabric away from Fort San Pedro and Plaza de Armas, a new orientation was given to the settlement's layout. The wide, straight roadways laid down in the suburbs were vital to this process. With their monumental axes running to/from public edifices such as the Capitol, they created clear sightlines to the city's democratic political institutions. All in all, the form of planning in Cebu and Zamboanga was repeated at smaller spatial scales in the provincial capitals during the 1910s and 1920s, for example, at Lingayen, Pangasinan Province – see Cameron (1914). By the 1920s, planning was wholly in the hands of Filipinos employed within the BPW's Division of Architecture (DoA).

It would be an error, as I have touched upon before, to think that City Beautiful-inspired planning was only undertaken in the Philippines by Americans. City Beautiful planning was evident in Manila and the provinces during the 1920s and

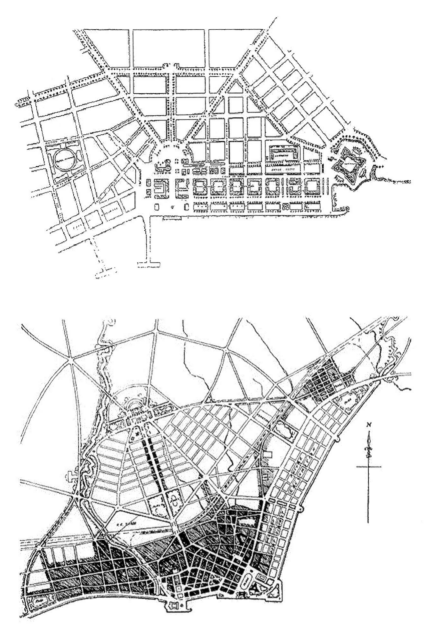

Figure 15 Top: William E. Parsons' city plan for Zamboanga, and (bottom) his
1912 plan for Cebu.

Source: A.N. Rebori (1917b).

1930s thanks to schemes composed by Filipinos employed within the DoA. In
fact, the visual imprint and volume of City Beautiful-inspired urban designing in
the Philippines pre-1941 was such that Thomas Hines (1972: 50) said its greatest

success was not on U.S. soil 'but on foreign colonial soil'. As mentioned earlier too, City Beautiful planning was solely done by Americans up to 1919. Yet, the identity of who undertook planning in the Philippines fundamentally shifted after that year. I will now give reference to historical context so to explain why this change occurred.

The year 1916 saw the passage of two political turning points. First, the Jones Act was passed. It was the first declaration of American intent to withdraw control of the Philippines and to recognize Philippine self-rule 'as soon as stable government can be established therein' (Malcolm, 1916: 741). In view of the new law's passing, the colonial civil service was Filipinized; colonial government positions were transferred from American to Filipino hands. Central to the new evolution in Philippine urban planning were Juan Arellano (1888–1960) and Antonio Toledo (1890–1972). Educated in the U.S., they had a hands-on role in developing planning activity in the Philippines before 1941.

Second, in December 1916, Act No. 2657 was passed. It reformed the organization, powers, and general administration of the colonial government, as well as emphasized the significance of planning to societal progress (Morley, 2019). Additionally, in 1918, Ralph Doane, the last American consulting architect, published an article titled 'Architecture in the Philippines'. Much overlooked in historiography, the text reveals the American understanding of the relationship between the advancement of art and the development of democracy in the Philippine Islands. Doane stresses that all 'progressive' and 'democratic' societies have their own architectural styles. He claims there is an immediate need for the invention of a 'Philippine style'.

To appreciate the importance of the colonial administration's Filipinization and the impact this had on offices such as the DoA, two matters must be borne in mind. On the one hand, the handover of power refashioned colonial policies in favour of Filipino priorities (Casteñeda Anastacio, 2016). In other words, Filipinization did not simply mean the replacement of personnel with Filipinos; it actually meant the empowerment of Filipinos for the first time to positions of core influence over the colonial regime. On the other hand, the Filipinos who rose to prominence after Filipinization, such as Arellano and Toledo, had participated in the Pensionados Program (following Act No. 854's passing in 1903) to receive advanced education in North America. Although radical nationalist historians in the Philippines have in the postcolonial context been successful in painting an image of Pensionados Program participants – 'pensionados' – as being both passive receptors of colonial education and bureaucracy, in truth the Filipinos who received higher education overseas were active participants in colonial education and, upon returning home, active contributors to colonial policy making. Paul Kramer (2006: 273) remarks that 'the most vocal expressions of nationalist colonialism came from *pensionados*'. However, notwithstanding their Beaux Arts training in the U.S. acting as the backbone of DoA activities from 1919, in the post-Act No. 2657 and Jones Act milieu Filipino architects were able to take on a much more involved and inventive role in shaping colonial government projects. Their innovation coincided with the new taste for imposing monumental edifices. These new public buildings incorporated design features referencing local people and their culture, and so whilst the structures might be labelled as 'colonial architecture', they actually advanced the narrative of proto-modern Filipino design borne out of the framework of Filipinization (Morley, 2024).

Against the backdrop of political reform, and the philosophical drive instigated by Doane to forge a 'legitimate' brand of native, modern architecture, by the early 1920s DoA schemes had become refashioned. Not only did architectural schemes include new forms of ornamentation and colour but the application of the City Beautiful in the Philippines also became laced with elements of Filipino nationalism. Given that, for the first time, public edifices and spaces were personalized with Filipino elements, 'buildings and spaces granted fresh reference points to endorse the existence and development of the Philippine nation, that is, a nation growing increasingly autonomous from the Americans' (Morley, 2018c: 256).

BPW archives in Manila shed much light on the evolution of the City Beautiful paradigm in the Philippines during the 1920s and 1930s. They reveal that three types of urban planning were practised: comprehensive city planning; the establishment of civic centres; and, the renewal of existing spaces (namely, the colonial Spanish plazas). Equal attention must be placed upon Act No. 3842, passed in December 1928. It allowed municipal governments to undertake urban planning as part of their broadening administrative remit (Morley, 2019). From thereon, municipalities equated the practice of planning with good local governance. As a result, from 1929, a flood of urban planning projects were undertaken by the BPW. The volume of plaza renewal projects, for example, surged.

In 1919, the first city plan composed by a Filipino was produced for Tayabas. Designed by Arcadio Arellano (1872–1920), the plan amalgamated a grid pattern of roads, arterial boulevards, monuments at the centre of public spaces, a park system, and commercial and civic districts. As a model of a modern, civic-minded Philippine settlement, Tayabas' plan inspired the DoA's Juan Arellano. In 1925, he produced plans for Calag-itan and San Jose in Antique Province, and in 1926 he produced his first plan for the major port of the Visayas Region, Iloilo.

Between 1926 and 1930, Juan Arellano revised his *Proposed Plan for the City of Iloilo and Vicinity*. As an early example of grand City Beautiful planning by a Filipino, the 1926 scheme demonstrates the fundamental environmental features comprising modern urban design in the Philippines. They are long, broad, straight roadways that connect districts together, symmetrically formed public spaces, and a symmetrically arranged civic centre. Later revisions of the city plan incorporate the siting of plazas, parks, and gardens in proximity to major thoroughfares. Parks and gardens are also sited along the banks of rivers and estuarine creeks (Morley, 2018c). The use of greenery, albeit along roadways, also forms a staple of Arellano's 1933 plan for Tagaytay.

During the American colonial era, provincial and municipal government buildings were built throughout the Philippines. From 1920 to 1929, as a point of illustration, more than 350 such edifices were built. The construction of provincial and municipal government buildings customarily involved the laying out of open space in proximity to the front elevation, and the bringing of the building and surroundings into direct association (Morley, 2019). Just as had occurred in Lingayen, in settlements such as Oroquieta (Misamis Occidental – see Figure 16), a roadway was laid out to directly correspond with the position of the government edifice's central section with main entrance. More so, in setting new classically-inspired Capitols and *Presidencias* (municipal administration offices) within sometimes extensive landscaped environments, for example, with flights of steps, a plaza, and double rows of trees marking the site boundary at the front, these edifices offered a new aesthetic highpoint in the evolution of provincial communities. They also physically accentuated the broad American desire to build democracy in all territories within the Philippine Archipelago.

Another major element of the Philippine City Beautiful was the redesign of Spanish colonial plazas. Labelled as Development Plans, the renewal of downtown plazas transpired as an outcome of broadening environmental management and local political ambition during the 1920s. As part of the revitalization of public spaces, new monuments dedicated to local or national heroes were built. Such architectural elements, often placed alongside fountains or bandstands, expose the growing sense of Philippine nationhood after the Jones Act was passed. Marking primary spatial alignments in public spaces, their siting often corresponds with nearby roadways so to terminate vistas as citizens approached the open plot. Thus bandstands, fountains, and monuments not only performed an aesthetic role of decorating an urban core's primary open area, they became a staple of Filipino urban planning exercises. Why? By 1920 the Philippine conception of Philippine democracy had widened. Statuary dedicated to champions of the Filipino quest for emancipation was proof, in Americans' eyes, of the readiness of the local population for future

Figure 16 A view of the driveway to the Misamis Occidental Provincial Capital in Oroquieta.

Source: The author.

self-government. Jazz bands playing in bandstands, to American eyes, revealed cultural advancement whilst the use of bandstands as soapboxes for public discussions of politics indicated growing Filipino awareness of civic responsibilities (Morley, 2019).

3.3 The Evolving Philippine City Beautiful: The Commonwealth Era (1935–46)

Earlier I emphasized that pre and post the Jones Act, the generic approach to urban planning in the Philippines adhered closely to Daniel Burnham's City Beautiful model. By 1935, with the commencement of the final phase of American colonial rule, the Philippine Government headed by President Manuel Quezon (1878–1944) planned a new capital city.

To be the postcolonial centre of the nation, Quezon City was to articulate the Filipino soul and epitomize native spirit and culture (Morley, 2023). With a layout originally composed by Harry Frost (1887–1943), Juan Arellano, and Alpheus Williams, the plan for Quezon City was purposefully to be distinct; it was to be exclusively Filipino in both form and meaning (Morley, 2023). President Quezon was central to the vision. He sought, notes Isabelo

Crisostomo (1971: 21), 'upang makapagtayo siya ng isang punong-lunsod o kabesera ng Pilipinas na natatangi sa kagandahan, kaayusan, katiwasayan at kaunlaran' (trans. *to build a capital city of the Philippines that is unique in its beauty, orderliness, security, and progress*), a place to be 'ang tagapagtanghal ng bansa – isang pook na libu-libong tao ang darating at dadalaw bilang linangan ng kultura at ng kaluluwa ng bansa' (Crisostomo, 1971: 9) (trans. *the showcase of the nation – a place where thousands would come and visit as the cradle of culture and the soul of the country*).

As a *truly* Filipino urban environment, Quezon City was to be allegedly better planned and more beautiful than Manila (Morley, 2023). It was to also show off the social ideals of the Commonwealth Government formed in 1935. Quezon City, in essence, was to express the power of the decolonizing Philippine state to provide 'modern communities where our laborers can live in a comfortable manner appropriate to their well-being' (Prudente Sta. Maria, 2010: 71). With boulevards and parkways, vast parks, and a grand civic core, the settlement, Michael Pante emphasizes (2019), was arguably the boldest urban planning scheme in Filipino history; this new environmental paradigm was to supply light, air, space, and greenery for all common people (*tao*). But, whereas in Manila the City Beautiful presence remained, in Quezon City modernist reasoning seeped in. The pre-World War Two development of Quezon City was a product of Filipino politicians and BPW staff thinking forwards: 'its physical form was shaped by their grasp of what a "good city" should be; and, its development symbolised efforts to promote national development on Filipino terms. It is the site where nationhood, monumentality, sense of place, and progressiveness became interdependent' (Morley, 2023: 87).

To claim that planning was an exclusively Quezon City-centred activity after the inauguration of the Commonwealth Era would be inaccurate. In Manila, from 1935 to 1941, Antonio Toledo was responsible for developing the cityscape of the Philippines' largest city. In 1939, he put forward schemes to renew Burnham's Sea Boulevard (today known as Roxas Boulevard), and at the urban fringe he suggested (in 1940) the construction of a wide circumferential roadway (Morley, 2023). For the district of Pandacan, Toledo composed a series of new roadways. To alleviate traffic congestion near the Manila Post Office he published the *Proposed Improvement around Plaza Lawton* (1940). He also redesigned other roadways in the city and laid out new approaches to bridges so that traffic flow could be enhanced. Furthermore, in 1938 and 1939, he composed the layout of parks in Malate. With symmetrical arrangements of lawns, trees, and hedges, the green spaces demonstrate Toledo's skill in civic art. Such capabilities were put on additional display via downtown architectural schemes, for example, the City Hall, the Department of Finance Building, and the

Agriculture and Commerce Building. These three edifices continued the development of the government district originally envisaged by Daniel Burnham and Peirce Anderson in 1905.

In the provinces Toledo, as well as Juan Arellano, designed public edifices and their surroundings. They also continued the revitalization of Spanish colonial plazas. Quite possibly, the epitome of the pre-war provincial projects was the 1937 scheme for the Municipal Building (later renamed City Hall) in San Pablo, Laguna. With the axis of the edifice's large entrance stairway directly corresponding to the alignment of a nearby roadway, a grand vista of the edifice was formed as one approached the building from downtown. Toledo's civic art skills, learnt originally at Ohio State University, enabled him to unite architectural elements on the building principal façade with the internal arrangement of rooms, and to the character of the surrounding built environment (Morley, 2023).

In summary, American colonization fundamentally reshaped the layout of towns and cities in the Philippine Islands. Whereas pre-1898 settlements were configured in accord with Spain's Laws of the Indies, following the importation of City Beautiful planning a new urban design paradigm took root. Focusing on tree-lined boulevards, green spaces, and grand vistas towards government offices, the practice of urban planning had morphed into the construction of suburban civic centres by the 1910s, and, by the 1920s, the redesign of Spanish colonial plazas. With City Beautiful practice continuing into the early 1940s, it is imperative not to underestimate the longevity and dispersion of City Beautiful urbanism in the Philippine Archipelago. The sheer volume of planning schemes meant in real terms that whilst the U.S. was ground zero for the inception of the City Beautiful planning type, the Philippines was the core practice point.

Discussed earlier in the Element, for most of the Philippines' City Beautiful era its practice was done by Filipinos, not Americans. Indeed, it may be argued that so ingrained was the City Beautiful planning model that the national planning system was wholly unready for societal conditions following the end of World War Two in 1945. By the commencement of Philippine national independence in July 1946, about 60 per cent of Manila's housing stock was still in ruins. The fact that American colonial planning had focused almost exclusively on civic art and spatial design, not housing and transport planning, meant urban reconstruction in the early postcolonial age was largely left to the private sector. The effect of this, heightened by rural-to-urban migration, caused urban densification to rapidly increase. Consequently, by the mid-1950s, Manila had an urban density greater than Manhattan Island in New York (Morley, 2023). Furthermore, at that time, the total amount of open space in Manila was just 1.79 square metres per person (Varias, 1955). This problem still plagues the metropolis today, and with slumlands on display throughout the built environment, the Philippine megacity now offers an environmental image contrasting greatly from that of Burnham's time. Manila today presents itself as a messy, even non-planned, city.

4 City Beautiful Planning and Nation-Building: Australia

Comparable to the Philippine context where the historiography of City Beautiful planning has traditionally focused almost exclusively on one individual, and a limited number of urban settlements, so too the written history of the City Beautiful in Australia has largely centred on one place, Canberra, and person, Walter Burley Griffin (1876–1937). Born in Illinois, and with work experience in Chicago, Griffin and his Canberra city plan had a profound impact on the evolving Australian planning framework.

In 1901, six formerly self-governing British colonies on the Australian subcontinent combined into a federal state. Griffin's plan for Canberra was laid down as an impressive expression of emergent Australian national sovereignty. Yet, in spite of Jeffrey Cody's (2003) belief that Griffin's work in Canberra bore little connection to American colonial planning in the Philippine Islands, in three principal ways it did. First, the plan of the Australian capital city adapted the construction of public buildings, spaces, and roads to the character of the natural landscape, as had earlier occurred in Manila and Baguio. Second, City Beautiful planning was employed in both the Philippines and Australia as fundamental components in governmental processes seeking to cultivate the local populations' formative sense of national identity (Morley, 2013). Third, similar to planning's development in the Philippine Islands, Australian planning during the early 1900s experienced profound revision. Discussed more fully subsequently in the Element, efforts were made in Australia to create more beautiful urban settlements. In embedding American City Beautiful planning within the context of Australia's formative planning movement, Freestone (2007b) shows that the basic tenets of modern American urban designing – the recognition of the visual and functional shortcomings of cities, the belief in social progress, the positive endorsement of urban life, the moral obligation to civic duty, the ameliorative power of beauty, the synthesis of utility and beauty, and so on – affected urban management and environmental design thinking 'down under'. Yet, he explains, what makes the Australian planning chronicle distinct is *how* the components of American City Beautiful philosophy resonated in the country.

Freestone (2007b) suggests that a country's inclination to implement the American City Beautiful planning model, and then refashion it to suit local needs, is influenced by how the social-design elements of City Beautiful ideology resonate within the national framework. This resonation of the elements, he explains, can occur singly and/or in different combinations. Gilbert A. Stetler (2000), more specifically, spells out that the making of a 'localized City Beautiful' is affected by two fundamental matters: the assumption that the urban core should have precedence in planning practice over the urban fringe; and, the breadth of the base for decision-making within a nation's urban planning process. In his view the City Beautiful was taken up outside of the U.S. because during the early 1900s, in many countries, planning professionalized.

4.1 1901: A New Nation Rises

If looking to uncover Australia's evolution from settler colony to self-governing nation, the story begins on 1 January 1901 with the Commonwealth of Australia Constitution Act. Given the watershed moment, the federation of six colonies into a single political-territorial entity 'meant that the new nation needed a national capital to represent its aspirations and to become the Seat of Government' (National Capital Authority, 2024). A capital city at Canberra (Figure 17) 'offered a perfect surface onto which the possibilities of the era could be projected' (Sonne, 2004: 149). Notably, from the outset, Canberra was to be a planned city. It was to be built on a scale hitherto unprecedented on the Australian subcontinent. In addition, the city's configuration of roads, open areas, and buildings were to integrate both utilitarian and symbolic elements so that, in the words of the 1912 federal capital competition design winner, Walter Burley Griffin (1913) (Figure 17), national sentiment and achievement could be expressed. Accordingly, to wholly comprehend what Canberra is, I claim it is necessary to consider its being from two dimensions: the city's physical form; and, its Australian environmental character (Morley, 2013). Owing to its 'Australian character', states Reps (1997), it is revealing to enquire *how* this disposition came about. Central to Canberra's 'Australianness', as I reveal in the Element, was the interplay between the built fabric and the natural landscape.

Paul Reid (2002) suggests that the design of Canberra mirrors the global development of city planning during the early 1900s. In fact, claims Robert Freestone (2007b: 80), 'to think of the city beautiful in Australia has been to think almost exclusively of Canberra, the biggest planning story of the early 20th century'. That said, other City Beautiful-type planning schemes were undertaken in Australia during the opening decades of the twentieth century. However, the legacy of the City Beautiful on Australian ground is somewhat diffuse. As Freestone makes clear, the character of City Beautiful-thought and practice assumed noticeable local variations (2007b: 80). Why? Churchward (1972) explains even with the apparent unity of political federation early-1900s

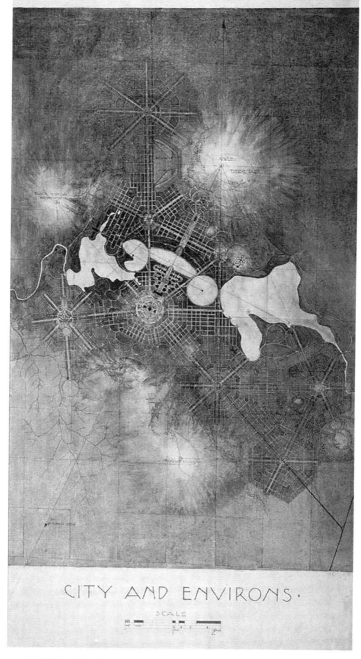

Figure 17 Walter Burley Griffin's prize-winning entry for the 1912 federal capital city design competition.

Source: National Archives of Australia (NAA): A710, 48.

Australia was still a 'fragmented society'. The country's states, for instance, had their own public administration systems and professional cultures. Basically, they operated relatively independently. This reality, coupled with Australia's enormous physical size, meant that in different areas of the country 'there was an unavoidable diversity in how planning needs and opportunities were interpreted'. In consequence, 'the character of city beautiful theorizing took on its own local variations' (Freestone, 1998: 99). Large-scale planning projects in Sydney, Melbourne, Perth, and elsewhere, whilst grounded in using Beaux Arts design, contained clear distinctions. As indicated earlier, a core reason for the variance lies with the fact that planners and government reformers worked 'independently in their own cities within their own respective realms – ceaseless propagandist activity, the state political arena, and local government administration' (Freestone, 1998: 100). The grandest City Beautiful articulation was, though, Griffin's Canberra plan.

Hailed in 1913 by influential Australian planner George Taylor as 'a progressionist' (1913: 46), Griffin was enmeshed in debates gripping Australian society post-independence about the roles of urban environments, nationalism, federalism, and social reform. In particular, following independent statehood and the constitutional need for a new capital city, debate raged over what the nation's new capital should be like. As the proverbial Eden of the fledgling nation, the capital city was invested with grand hopes: *it was to be the most beautiful of the modern world*. In accomplishing this goal, Freestone (2007b) has observed that particular metaphors were regularly employed within Australian planning discourse, and they evoked themes plucked straight out of the American City Beautiful songbook: 'artistic', 'picturesque', 'beautiful', 'stately', and 'commodious'.

With 137 proposals submitted for the 1912 planning competition, Griffin's winning entry presented 'the undeniable hallmarks of a classic city beautiful plan. It was extravagant, formal, geometric, and artistically produced' (Freestone, 2007b: 85). With planning influenced by the natural environment, Griffin's scheme permitted future urban growth far beyond the original population limit of 25,000 people. More so, being born at a time when urban planning was 'no longer a new or experimental endeavour but one that had made much progress in places such as North America and Europe' (Reps, 1997: 9), the city plan 'combined several specialized centres arranged in circular, hexagonal, or octagonal road systems. Radial thoroughfares link these centres located on both sides of a chain of lakes. Topography largely determined the pattern of the central triangular composition' (Reps, 1997: 140).

The siting of the city's most important edifices, and by extension, the nation's most important buildings, for example the House of Parliament, the homes of the governor-general and prime minister, was determined in accordance with

Figure 18 Marion Mahoney Griffin's perspective sketch of the view southwest
from the summit of Mount Ainslie.

Source: PIC/9929/562 LOC Album 1092/1 National Library of Australia.

Griffin's understanding of Australian democracy (Taylor, 1914; Figure 18). The
buildings were sited in central positions accessible from all parts of the city, and
as a result to be readily seen. This, Griffin thought, would make the public feel
'close' to the nation's high offices and the officers of government.

George Taylor's *Town Planning for Australia* (1914) and John Sulman's *An
Introduction to the Study of Town Planning in Australia* (1921) clarify the
nascent character of modern urban planning in Australia. Both publications
offer much analysis of the ideas and practices of 'effective' urban designing past
and present. Taylor (1914), for instance, suggests a 'good plan' is inspired by
a planner's imagination, and Sulman (1849–1934) bluntly highlights the limited
value of grid plans that had typified Australia's colonial age. Rather, he remarks
(1921), against the backdrop of federalism and enlarging public demands upon
the state, the form of an urban plan should depend not only on economic,
cultural, health, and infrastructure interests but on the *kind* of urban settlement
in question. Hence,

> in a political capital like Washington, or that proposed at Canberra, the
> Government buildings and public offices are the chief features, and should
> be so grouped and disposed that they would afford the maximum of conveni-
> ence in intercommunication between departments; and at the same time by
> their stateliness and dignity, should typify the sense of power and order which
> is at the root of all stable government. (Sulman, 1921: 28)

Commenting further of Canberra, Sulman recognized the distinctiveness of the
city's site/the local natural environment. He identified (1921: 28) its influence upon
the character of the Australian capital even though, by the early 1920s,
a Washington, D.C.-type 'spacious central parkway' had been laid out. Sited at

Figure 19 A view north from Red Hill to Mount Ainslie with, in the foreground, the present-day Australian Parliament Building and, in the background, Anzac Parade and the Australian War Memorial at the foot of Mount Ainslie.
Source: The author.

the front of the Parliament House, it corresponded with a similar type of open area (today known as the Anzac Parade) on the opposite/northern shore of the centrally located lake (see Figure 19). Taylor (1914), similar to Sulman, perceived Canberra's site and scenic beauty as a key trait in making the settlement unique in Australian city building. In his view, Canberra is an ideal Australian city.

4.2 Canberra: An Ideal City in the Australian Landscape

Just as in the U.S., where City Beautiful planning was driven by the promotion of aesthetics, the same was considered in Australia to be a pillar of modern urban planning. In implementing a 'beautiful city' in Australia, public buildings were massed around open spaces and water features were exploited. In the 1905 Manila Plan, Burnham and Anderson united key public edifices and roadways with the Pasig River, estuarine inlets, and Manila Bay; and, in the 1909 Plan of Chicago, Daniel Burnham and Edward Bennett had suggested linking the site of cultural institutions with green spaces and the shoreline of Lake Michigan. Similarly, in Canberra, the inner districts were to be laid out around a substantially sized lake (later named Lake Burley Griffin). Thus, in these three cities, the built fabric and water features were to be brought into unity. However, in the case of Canberra the relationship between built fabric and landscape was reinforced by the utilization of the surrounding 'amphitheatre of hills'. With two major planning alignments – the land axis, and the water axis – demonstrating the attempt by Griffin to integrate the built environment with the natural setting, Canberra's plan was, to cite Paul Reid (2002), a fusion of Australian pragmatism with Chicago idealism. Nicholas Brown (2014), in fortifying Reid's point, judged Canberra to voice the nature of the Australian countryside in association with the nature of the Australian democratic experience.

To strengthen comparison between urban planning in the U.S., the Philippine Islands, and Australia during the early 1900s, notwithstanding the Philippines having a lengthy colonial history and regime change at the end of the nineteenth century, in the U.S. and Australia entrenched architectural communities existed. Each, for example, had their own publications. In contrast, in the Philippines, at least until the 1920s, no officially licensed architectural and planning profession existed, civic planning organizations were few and far between, and sources of information regarding planning practice was essentially limited to 'official outlets', namely Bureau of Insular Affair reports, annual reports of the Director of Public Works, or the Bureau of Public Works' *Quarterly Bulletin*. In the case of Australia, journals helped propagate the understanding that the City Beautiful's influence went far beyond the North American continent (Freestone, 2007b: 46). In essence, thanks to journals and widening discourse among Australian designers and politicians, 'the term city beautiful helped organise and consolidate moves toward civic improvement'. More so, states Freestone (2007b), there is a need within studies of the City Beautiful's internationalization to move away from the standpoint that it only diffused to countries through top-down political channels, i.e. as it did from the U.S. to the Philippines. He declares that the City Beautiful's international diffusion owed much to professional and bureaucratic enterprises, and populist initiatives sponsored by civic and commercial organizations.

The Australian experience of the City Beautiful to a great extent mirrored many dynamics evident in the U.S., where planning happened at a variety of environmental scales. In Australia, planning schemes ranged from the small-sized, for example, individual public spaces, through to the redesign of metropolitan downtowns and the composing of a new capital city. Even though Griffin's Canberra project borrowed heavily from Burnham's City Beautiful vision, it was seen from the outset to be an Australian *not* American urban place.

Canberra's location merged five environmental features: tree-covered hills at a distance from downtown; three mountains within the city limits (i.e., Mounts

Ainslie, Mugga Mugga, and Black Mountain); the Molonglo River (and basin); the gentle undulating land throughout the city site; and, the lower hills within the river valley (Pegrum, 2008: 134). The natural environment, observes Ken Taylor (2007: 17), 'has a meaning and significance that communicate what Canberra is'. Because the natural surroundings are a signifier of place and likewise grant *identity with place*, not only was Griffin's plan helping to forge a better society for Australians, it was also bestowing a revered vision of 'the bush'. Yet, landscape alone did not make the urban plan become Australian.

For Griffin, his city plan had to allow for Australian democratic expression (Headon, 2003). The opinion that Griffin held was that Australia had little history of self-rule yet it possessed strong democratic tendencies and bold government. As a place with a 'great future', and it being country wholly willing to 'fully express the possibilities for individual freedom, comfort and convenience for public spirit' (Griffin, 1913: 65–66), the Canberra plan's centrepiece both in physical and representational terms was the Government Group. Here, states Taylor (2007: 48), 'the symbolic role of the landscape setting of Canberra, with the grand view of Parliament sweeping down the great land axis to focus on the dominant mass of Mount Ainslie with the replicated effect of Black Mountain to the west, is palpable'. Of the mountains, they terminate the principal planning axes and offer important vistas. The realized city exhibits nature 'as a spatial container and crucible of symbolic meaning' (Vernon, 2010b: 135).

Whilst Griffin's city plan has been rightly lauded for the picturesque urban environment it produced, it is easy to overlook that his interpretation of the City Beautiful planning model helped to emphasize the value of Canberra's natural setting as a *critical public landscape*. In view of this, Canberra must be recognized not only as a practical exercise in comprehensive urban planning but also as an example of *critical practice* because it sought to yield new urban environmental results within the Australian urban context. In venturing to deal with practical problems within Australian society in order to uplift citizens' well-being, and in seeking to express Australian identity, Griffin's Canberra layout purposefully 'spoke' of both the worldly and the representational. Griffin presented a new model of urban design to the country so as to provoke, define, and mold change within the institutional, material, and representational domains of Australian life. The character of his city plan was new to the country but, significantly too, it was grounded in its cultural and political realities. Monumentalizing nature, in part as a response to his knowledge of pre-Burnham planned Chicago where largely unregulated urban expansion ate away at the rural surrounds, Griffin 'envisaged Canberra as a design alternative to urban indifference to the natural world' (Vernon, 2010b: 135).

4.3 The City Beautiful in the Provinces

City Beautiful-inspired planning projects occurred in Australia's largest provincial settlements as well as in the new city of Canberra. However, it must be made clear that the City Beautiful model was relevant to Australia before the 1912 federal capital design competition, as evidenced by the 1909 *Report of the Royal Commission for the Improvement of the City of Sydney and its Suburbs* ('*Report of the Royal Commission*'). Remarks Freestone (2007b), the *Report of the Royal Commission* brought new aesthetic values to the Australian planning system although the role of beautification was very much secondary to other concerns at that time. The 1909 report, he said (2007b: 128), nevertheless 'represented a watershed in Sydney's planning history, integrating incremental, ad hoc moves towards city improvement into a general stock-take of recommendations which established a foundation for successive rounds of public investment and reformist endeavour'. It 'remains one of the most internationally-informed of all modern planning reports for Sydney' (Freestone, 2007b: 124).

In Sydney, and in other urban settlements in Australia, to generalize, the absorbing of overseas planning knowledge and models took three basic forms: the foreign precedent as a positive model: 'something inspirational to emulate'; the negative model: 'an example to be avoided'; and the rhetorical: 'an acknowledgement of foreign initiative but a conviction that Sydney could do better' (Freestone, 2007b: 125). Vital to the growth of local knowledge was the importation of foreign planning literature, and, as already mentioned, the publication of Australian journals and books. Taking the example of the periodical *Building* (founded in 1907), it shifted awareness of the benefits of urban beauty to a point in the years immediately after its founding that planning was widely viewed as a societal asset.

In further emphasizing the significance of the 1909 Royal Commission report, it referenced park systems as well as road and public spaces layouts in the U.K., continental Europe, and the U.S. as part of the ongoing Western crusade to revamp cities. Giving attention to contemporary American planning schemes, for example, Burnham and Bennett's 1905 San Francisco Plan and the 1907 New York City Improvement Commission Plan, the 1909 report inspired new ideas and projects to improve Sydney's urban condition. These included John Sulman's recommendation of a monumental boulevard leading to/from the ferry terminus at Circular Quay (see Figure 20). Stressing the value of urban environmental order and spaciousness, the aforementioned report and subsequent proposals demonstrated that in Australia, other than at Canberra, City Beautiful ideas were 'integral but not touchstone' (Freestone, 2007b: 136). The generic value of the City Beautiful, as presented by means of the dozens of

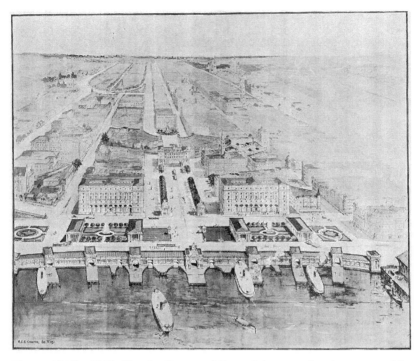

Figure 20 The 1909 Circular Quay and Central Avenue planning proposal by
John Sulman.

Source: *Report of the Royal Commission* (1909).

plans/reports for American cities during the early 1900s (Peterson, 2003), was,
however, threefold: it granted a model of comprehensive city planning
to Australian professionals; it provided a methodology in order to avoid a
piece-by-piece approach to urban design; and, it underscored the need within
evolving Australian city planning to ensure that the artistic side of urban design
was represented (Freestone, 2007b).

The artistic component of Australian planning found expression during the
1910s and the 1920s in state capitals such as Melbourne, Sydney, and Perth. In
1921 John Sulman presented a grand civic centre proposal for Sydney. Sulman
states (1921: 80) that the establishing of a civic centre augments civic esteem
given that 'civic pride is the basis of all civic progress'. This proposal though
should not be viewed in isolation because during the early 1920s Alexander
Macdonald recommended redeveloping Melbourne's south bank of the River
Yarra. Sulman described this particular scheme as a 'good plan for a civic
centre' (Sulman, 1921: 78). Likewise, in Perth, with support of the city council,
Carl Klem (1883–1952) made recommendations for grouping local and state

government and cultural buildings. His scheme explicitly demonstrated contemporary American influence.

Outside of state capitals, large-sized civic centre projects for provincial settlements were somewhat rare, but Geelong, in Victoria, is a standout exception. Implemented during World War One to a design composed by Percy Everett (1888–1967), Geelong's new civic quarter demonstrated what was possible for provincial urban environmental beautification (Freestone, 2010). Equally, while new parks and downtown public spaces were built in localities throughout Australia, their implementation was judged through three values: the social, the economic, and the aesthetic. Australia's planning trends by 1915 – notwithstanding Canberra – exceeded the City Beautiful paradigm. Planning *had* to be practical and by 1917, at the first national planning conference in Adelaide, this was the perspective held by influential persons including Charles Reade (1880–1933), David Davidson (1893–1952), and James Barrett (1862–1945). Such a standpoint did not hinder the establishment of local improvement associations though, but the Great Depression during the 1930s truly rang the death knell for the Australian City Beautiful Movement. From thereon artistic urban designing was never a core objective of Australian urban designing. Yet, civic centres remained in the post-war era an enduring ideal 'albeit generally moving away from the beaux arts ideal.' (Freestone, 2007b: 164).

In conclusion, in the years immediately after federation, civic beautification was a visible element of the Australian urban design roadmap. But, besides Canberra where it produced 'a highly artistic masterpiece of great town planning expertise' (Fischer, 1989: 162), it was *not* the key driver of city planning. Beauty though *was* appreciated as long as it was able to support other societal advancement functions. Plus, given the fiscal challenges in underwriting expensive planning projects, Australian urban designers downsized the monumentality of the American City Beautiful planning model to a more modest practice of laying out individual public edifices within unencumbered sites. In consequence, few American-type civic centres were implemented as originally planned. The staple of the democratically-minded Australian urban planner's daily operation was, quite simply, to ensure the supply to the public of more air, light, and happiness 'in homes and lives' (Taylor, 1914: 6).

5 China and the Advent of Large-Scale Modern City Planning

In the first half of the twentieth century, American architects, planners, construction firms, and real estate development companies were among the troupe of international personalities, entrepreneurs, and businesses who sought profits from an ever-changing China (Cody, 2003). From 1905, the presence of American architects was felt in Shanghai. During the Republican Era (1912–49) their stamp became apparent in other cities. Why this influence was able to proliferate throughout the country, and in doing so shape modern Chinese urban design thinking and practice, a handful of matters must be acknowledged.

From the late 1800s and through the first half of the twentieth century, China's urbanization increased. A key reason for urban growth was the economy's industrial development. In association, cityscapes acquired an altered layout and appearance: 'local elites and government officials experimented with different ideas about how to plan, construct, and manage cities' (Lincoln, 2021: 175). To support this process was a cast of architects and planners, mostly Chinese but some foreign. As to the background of the Chinese professionals, dozens of them had received higher education in the United States (U.S.) as a result of the Boxer Indemnity Scholarship Program's (庚子賠款獎學金) establishment in 1908. Significantly too, alongside their domestically educated counterparts and the foreign experts, they pooled up-to-date national and international concepts and practices about how China's cities could be built and planned. In particular, through holding teaching positions at universities and as employees of urban administrations, the U.S.-educated Chinese promoted the need for modern urban designing in their homeland (Lincoln, 2021). Aiding the proliferation of information as to how societal improvement could occur, and thereby widening opportunity for discussion of urban environmental planning, were new publications and vocational organizations.

In 1928 the Chinese Architects Association (中國建築師學會) was founded. Many of its forty-plus original members were educated in Europe and the U.S. They included Lu Yen-Chih (呂彥直, 1894–1929), Dong Dayou (董大酉, 1899–1973), Fan Wenzhao (范文照, 1893–1979), and Yang Tingbao (楊廷寶, 1901–1982), who respectively received architectural education at Cornell University, Columbia University, and the University of Pennsylvania. Being key individuals with regard to the designing of public edifices, public spaces, and urban districts 'along modern American lines', their professional activities occurred against the backdrop of urban government reform; in 1921 and 1928 new laws on urban administration were passed. Explains Stapleton (2007), the combination of governmental reorganization, educational expansion, and evolution in urban culture allowed new philosophies to emerge about the Chinese city, its design, and the betterment of citizens' lives. Such intellectualism was typified by Hankou's municipal administrator, Dong Xiujia (董修甲). He, in the late 1920s, 'celebrated the rise of the city as China's best hope for the future' (Stapleton, 2007: 72). Of additional note, emphasizes Joseph Esherick (1999), new concepts of city administration and urban design were not only embraced but largely accepted/understood along the same lines. In fact, states Stapleton

(2022a: 31), even in regions afflicted by military conflict the warlords 'tended to regard visually impressive cities as critical to establishing their legitimacy as modern political leaders'.

To augment understanding of why modern urban planning occurred in China, Kristin Stapleton's (2022b) paper in the journal *Twentieth-Century China* demands review. In 'The Rise of Municipal Government in Early-Twentieth Century China: Local History, International Influence, and National Integration', she dissects changes in governance albeit with attention to the scale of municipal organization. Among Stapleton's core findings are that transformation to the organizational size of municipal statecraft during the 1920s modified the character of urban governance. In the context of an age when national politics was fragmented, the Nationalist government was reversing the administrative decentralization established during the late Qing Dynasty (1644–1911), and cities were increasingly perceived as 'territorial units' within the political economy, the expansion of urban territorial boundaries and the catering of swelling populations permitted a need for municipal administrations to devise new 'scale strategies'. Such need set in motion potential to, as an example, absorb overseas metropolitan planning models. Subsequently, the Element will reveal that models other than the American City Beautiful were evident in China. However, before discussing non-American planning types, attention is given to the importation of the American City Beautiful planning model.

5.1 Henry Murphy: The U.S.' Central Planning Agent in China

An American protagonist central to the development of modern Chinese city planning was Henry Murphy (1877–1954). Against the backdrop of the Republican government seeking to instigate municipal reforms as part of national construction (國家建設), Murphy's work in Guangzhou was particularly influential.

As the Republic Era unfolded, two major transitions occurred as to how Chinese cities were managed. In the opening decade of the Republican Era, especially in the south of China, municipal governments were remodelled on American prototypes. In this context, by the second decade of the Republic Era, they began to 'refashion the physical aspects of their cities with American precedents in mind' (Cody, 2001: 174). Henry Murphy found himself at the axis of transition in Chinese municipal politics and city planning. Taking forward the modernized vision of Guangzhou envisaged by Mayor Sun Ke (孫科, 1891–1973), son of Sun Yat-sen (孫中山, 1866–1925) and a graduate of politics and city planning at Columbia University and the University of California Los Angeles, Murphy was able to build upon the city's new charter (issued in March 1921). Subsequently new attention was put

upon land development, industrial growth, the improvement of traffic circulation, the removal of decrepit edifices, and the development of urban infrastructure. Post-1921, the city was organized and governed as a city in the U.S. would
be; not only were detached California-style single-family residences constructed in the new suburbs, at the urban core boulevards were laid out, new
public spaces formed, memorials constructed, and a large-sized civic centre
built (Far Eastern Review, 1931b: 352–355). The design of new memorials was
said to reveal 'Chinese architecture according to the principles of aesthetics
and it is neither the adapting of Chinese forms to modern construction nor *vice
versa*' (Lu, 1929a: 99).

As a gauge of post-Qing Dynasty/early-Republican Era societal progress,
Guangzhou was to articulate advancement through the modernization of its
infrastructure, its changed cityscape with broad thoroughfares and free-flowing
traffic, and the enacting of a progressive grasp of municipal governance. Such
matters came to a head in early 1927 with Murphy's comprehensive plan for the
city. Two features define the character of the urban planning scheme: the
revitalization of the harbour facilities – a matter to be undertaken with assistance from Ernest Goodrich (1874–1955); and the establishing of a civic centre,
that is, an environmental feature that 'had become commonplace in many large
American cities as a result of the ideals expressed by Daniel Burnham and
others at the turn of the century' (Cody, 2003: 116). At the time it was made
public, *The New York Times* (1927) recorded that Murphy's scheme comprised
of a grand central axis, a boulevard parallel to the river, and a civic core from
which radiate four boulevards. Their axes were aligned to prominent monuments so that 'long vistas' could be produced to and from the architectural
objects (and to the mountains behind them – thereby capturing *feng shui* for
good local fortune (Meyer, 1978)). In summary, the 1927 Guangzhou Plan
synthesized 'the urban planning ideals of the City Beautiful Movement with
those of axial symmetry in places such as the Forbidden City in Beijing' (Cody,
2003: 117).

As impressive as Murphy's planning proposal for Guangzhou was, it somewhat paled in comparison to the plans for Nanjing. Given the status of the
capital city of Republican China in 1927, Murphy was hired in the
following year as an advisor to the National government. In view of the political
regime's belief that a well-designed capital city would invoke a sense of China's
proud past, plus articulate Sun Yat-sen's revolutionary vision for his nation and
its modernization under the hand of the Guominndang (国民党) (Chinese
Social and Political Science Review, 1930; Denison and Ren, 2008), Chinese
architectural firms were invited to submit designs. Nine did, and these were
published in late 1929. Curiously, all plans contained the same environmental

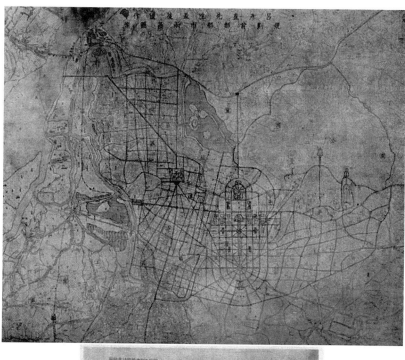

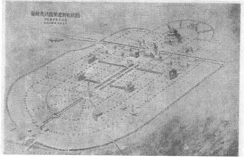

Figure 21 Top: Lu Yen Chih's proposed plan for Nanjing, and (bottom) the proposed plan for the capital city's urban core.

Source: *Liangyou Pictorial* (1929a) and *Liangyou Pictorial* (1929b).

elements: a grid layout punctured by long diagonal boulevards and a large open mall such as the one in Washington, D.C. (Musgrove, 2013). The American influence upon Chinese planning thought was unmistakably evident in the Draft Outline Plan for the Capital Metropolitan Area by Lu Yen Chih (規劃首都都市區圖案大綱草案 呂彥直遺著) (Figure 21). Referencing the planning exemplars of Haussmann's Paris and L' Enfant's Washington, D.C., Lu remarked of the need in China to learn from the planning heritage of Europe and the U.S. (Lu, 1929b: 1).

Although none of the submitted city plans for Nanjing were selected for implementation (largely due to cost – the city budget was ¥6 million versus bids in the range of ¥15–20 million), the competition judges opined that grand urban design would generate patriotic feeling and impress foreign visitors. Yet, whilst Chinese designers took inspiration from Western environmental models, they did not follow foreign planning precedents blindly (Tsui, 2011). In other words, China's modernization and environmental reformation would, states Charles Musgrove (2013: 100), 'not simply be a matter of imitating the West'. What is clear though, at least in the view of Musgrove (2013: 102), was that the proposals for Nanjing's administrative core 'resembled designs for the City Beautiful movement'.

5.2 The Greater Shanghai Civic Centre

In the frame of the effort during the Republican Era to reshape society's general form (Denison and Ren, 2008), the U.S. was perceived as a model for modern municipal urban governance and the practice of urban planning. With 'groups of enthusiasts' in the fields of city administration, architecture, civil engineering, and planning having received education in the U.S., Henry Murphy was able to directly introduce planning concepts and practices that modernized the Chinese built fabric without wiping out architectural heritage and traditional notions of beauty. In particular, Guangzhou demonstrated that environmental moderniza-tion could be instigated without destroying a city's authentic charm. New roads, for example, could align with the position of mountains, and aged temples could be preserved. As Tony Atkin (2011) explained, in the 1920s and 1930s China endeavoured to learn from Western methods in order to reform the country. A distinct sense of modernity emerged: on one hand, it encouraged the continu-ation of Chinese 'form'; yet, on the other hand, it adapted Western 'content'. This syncretic amalgam of architectural styles, said by Jianfei Zhu (1998: 4) to be something 'like a 'Chinese Beaux Arts', was to become known as 'Chinese Renaissance Architecture' (Far Eastern Review, 1931a; Zhang, 2022).

Other than Guangzhou and Nanjing, the influence of contemporary American urbanism was evident in settlements such as Shanghai. In 1929 Dong Dayou proposed a Beaux Arts-influenced plan for the Greater Shanghai Civic Center (GSCC). As a key member of China's first generation of modern architects, the Columbia University-educated Dong's vocational endeavours 'encapsulate the profound cultural pathos and political vicissitudes that he and his generation had to navigate' (Kuan, 2011: 169). Although the civic district's initial design – said to echo the City Beautiful layouts tendered for St. Louis and Denver – was composed by Zhao Shen (赵深, 1898–1978), a graduate of the University of

Pennsylvania, the scheme was rejected due to the lack monumentality and lack of appreciation 'of the full possibilities of Chinese architecture and knowledge of how to adapt it to the practical requirements of modern city planning and construction' (Far Eastern Review, 1930: 297).

In revising the GSCC plan, Dong recommended a layout of public edifices arranged alongside two enormous axes with their point of intersection marked by a fifty-metre-high pagoda. With one axis marked by a 2,000-foot-long reflecting pool, the grandeur and scale of the planning scheme with its open spaces, water features, and dozen-plus structures 'had no obvious precedent in premodern Chinese building practice' (Kuan, 2011: 173). The scheme alluded to the influence of Washington, D.C.'s cityscape upon evolving Chinese urban design theory and practice. Such an approach to planning at the urban core was explained by Dong (1935: 106): 'monumental buildings can only be seen to advantage if they are approached by streets of adequate width and length affording a view of them from distance', and the 'advantage of grouping the public buildings is not only to permit the concentration of public business and facilitate the conduct of inter-bureau affairs but also to add dignity to the city and impress visitors'.

About the rest of Shanghai, Dong's scheme incorporated major new thoroughfares, including sixty-metre-wide boulevards and thirty-metre-wide arterial roadways (Far Eastern Review, 1931a). Shen Yi (1933), a government official overseeing the restructuring of Shanghai in the 1930s, identified the European models of Paris, Berlin, and Moscow, *and* newly planned cities such as Canberra upon the laying out of Shanghai's new road system. He remarked upon the need in Shanghai to construct a spider web road plan, that is, a road configuration like that in the Australian capital ('有主張採用蜘蛛網式者, 若莫斯科及澳洲都城堪培拉之道路系統.'), and that '我人均知都市設計之完美與否, 與道路之佈置' (trans. '*the perfection of urban design is closely related to the layout of roads*').

Other than grand city plans, and equally grand schemes to construct new civic centres, the influence of the City Beautiful was apparent elsewhere in China. A standout example is the campus of Fukien Christian University (福建協和大學), designed by Henry Murphy (in 1918), and the proposed civic centre in Suzhou. Composed in 1929 by Liu Shiyang (柳士英, 1893–1973), the civic plan came about as an upshot of local political development and the provision of new funds to allow the municipal administration to employ, for the first time, a planning professional (Carroll, 2011). Explains Cody (1996: 368), notwithstanding Guangzhou, Nanjing, and Shanghai being the vanguard of the new metropolitan paradigm, 'other urban administrators throughout China in the 1920s and early 1930s, either consciously or unwittingly "Americanized" their cities to varying extents'.

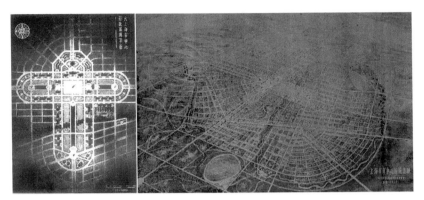

Figure 22 Left: Dong Dayou's plan for the Greater Shanghai Civic Centre
(GSCC), and (right) a bird's eye perspective of Shanghai and the GSCC.
Sources: *The Chinese Architect* (1934) and *Shanghai Youth* (1933).

5.3 Non-American Planning Influence in China (i): Socialist City Planning

Earlier in the Element I referenced city planning influences from other than from
the U.S. were evident in China. As will now be shown, Soviet planning (*ggrados-
troitel'stvo*) offered a competing vision of grand urban design to the City Beautiful.

A detailed inquiry of city planning history within the socialist political context
has been carried out by Katherine Zubovich (2024). Her findings reveal that before
World War Two 'socialist cities existed in the Soviet Union alone' (Zubovich,
2024: 6). However, post-1945, and analogous to the international spread of the
American City Beautiful during the early 1900s, the Socialist City planning
model's diffusion led to its adaption in different geographical and cultural settings,
that is, in parts of Africa, Asia, Europe, and Latin America. Zubovich's exploration
of Soviet planning's international propagation in many respects underpins Stephen
Ward's earlier studies on the relatedness to, and impacts of, foreign planning
models upon national planning movements. He remarks (2018) that international
knowledge circulation is a key part of the planning's evolution yet there is still
much to learn as to how urban design ideas and practices become imported and
sustained. Quite possibly, to grant explanation of the initial Soviet planning
footprint on Chinese soil there is need to know of Chinese knowledge concerning
pre-World War Two on-the-ground urban design experimentation in Russia
(Crawford, 2022), which itself was affected by overseas urban planning theory
(Clark, 2011; Thomas, 1978). It is therefore very likely that Chinese planners knew
of the monumental Moscow General Plan. It was 'the best-known planning project
of the prewar Stalinist period' (Taylor and Kukina, 2018: 197).

As I have just mentioned, Soviet planning was initially fashioned under the influence of Western urban design theories. Significantly, the Soviet planning model was not ignored in the West and had influence within the planning communities of Britain and the U.S. From the 1930s to 1960s, for example, the British planning movement was swayed by Soviet planning rationalism and utopianism (Ward, 2012), and in the U.S., at least in the 1920s and 1930s, Soviet planning was of interest. Numerous parallels in the form of city planning in the Soviet Union and in the U.S. existed even though, from the perspectives of doctrine, administration, and architectural character, contrasts were observable. The same is true of China. As to why city managers in the country, for example, during the 1920s and 1930s, acquired knowledge of Soviet planning, Osborn and Reiner (1962) suggest that all modernizing nations share a common goal. It is to develop their industrial economy whilst safeguarding welfare for citizens through the form of urban fabrics.

Published in 1935, and building upon early-1930s urban developments such as the construction of the underground train system and the laying out of new residential districts in Moscow, the Moscow General Plan comprised of numerous planning elements although a fundamental was road design/layout: 'A whole series of new streets and radial thoroughfares will be laid out; old squares will be widened, new squares will be laid out, crooked thoroughfares will be eliminated; narrow streets will be decidedly broadened' (Union of Soviet Architects, 1935: 5). Seeking to remove the environmental 'chaos' of Moscow's historic built fabric, from the point of view of architecture the 'new city' was to have uniformly designed streets, public spaces, and river embankments. The General Plan's report outlined the decisive role of Soviet architecture. It was to create 'mighty urban ensembles, each subject to a definite architectural idea and in their totality constituting the body of the socialist city' (Union of Soviet Architects, 1935: 6).

A widely acknowledged turning point in the Soviet-Chinese urban planning narrative was the year 1949; Russian experts arrived in China to share their experiences. With the establishment of the Communist state on 1 October 1949, during the following ten years Soviet specialists assisted the Chinese in developing their own socialist planning system. This agency was to be especially profound in Beijing. The 1953 plan, for example, proposed a new system of roads ranging from 40 to 100 metres in width. Plus, to underscore the symbolic importance of the new communist state, the city centre became the site for central government offices (Sit, 1996). Such strategy highlighted the contrast in Chinese and Soviet planning. Whilst socialist city planning as practiced in Russia stressed the need for an absolute rupture from the design of pre-socialist cities, China's Mao-era urban planning did not. Even in industrial settlements such as Anshan in Manchuria, which was occupied by the

Japanese from 1918 to 1945, a continuity with the past was maintained within the built fabric. Wholesale urban demolition and rebuilding was not undertaken as a matter of course (Hirata, 2023).

Hao Li (2022), by examining the Soviet imprint upon the development of large-sized provincial cities, for example, Shanghai, Shenyang, Xi'an, Baotou, Lanzhou, Luoyang, and Hangzhou during the era 1949 to 1959, confirms the similarity of planning activity across the country. Even though, as Zubovich (2024: 35) observes, the Soviet planning model had substantial impact upon both Chinese architecture and urban management, the Soviets in China viewed modern cities in the country with 'real difference'. Li (2022) confirms this; he identifies that a localization of the Soviet planning model transpired.

In his inquiry of large-scale plans in large-sized provincial cities, Li references the thoughts and deeds of planners such as the Russian named Muhkin (穆欣). Li recognizes that foreign planning professionals were sensitive to China's conditions, so when composing plans they 'often cited Chinese cases and urban construction traditions in Beijing, Tianjin, and Chengdu'. This actuality, Li adds, demonstrates that in the process of importing Soviet planning theory and practice into China, Mukhin and his peers were 'influenced by Chinese urban construction, cultural tradition, and contemporary construction practice' (Li, 2022: 828–829). However, as to why 1959 was a turning point in the Soviet-Chinese planning chronicle, Li states that Soviet planners' visits to China came to an end and major ideological differences had emerged between the Soviet and Chinese political leaders. With the Great Leap Forward (大跃进) in 1958, Chinese communist leader Mao Zedong (毛泽东, 1893–1976) demanded a planning system more in tune with local contexts (Li, 2022). Such nativist outlook for the evolution of Chinese planning produced high-points by the mid-1960s, for example, the development of the industrial city of Daqing. Daqing's planning, analyses Hou Li (2018), not only transformed the settlement into China's premier oil refining centre but enabled it to become an ideal model of Maoist industrial and urban environmental development.

5.4 Non-American Planning Influence in China (ii): Japan's Occupation

Japanese influence upon the design of urban environments in China should not be under estimated. The reshaping of Japanese life during the Meiji Era (1868–1912), and the development of the Japanese empire, profoundly affected the nature of urban planning activity in Manchuria as well as in Taiwan and the Korean Peninsula. Within these territories grand colonial capitals, for example, Hsinking (today known as Changchun), Taipei, and Seoul, were formed to articulate Japanese imperial authority. However, it must be spelt out that Japanese influence was apparent in China in other ways. If dozens of Chinese students were known from the late Qing Dynasty to have studied architecture, planning, and municipal administration in the U.S., then likewise it must be understood that 100s if not thousands of young persons received their education in Japan. As to why planning historiography (in English, at least) has tended to overlook such persons, the answer might be best answered by Abidin Kusno in *The Routledge Handbook of Planning History* (2018). He suggests that within studies of planning history, particularly with regard to Asia and the effects of modernization and colonization, attention has almost wholly focused upon East–West relations and not inter-Asian affairs. As such, Japan's occupation of various parts of Asia during the early mid-1900s has to a great degree been ignored within the writing of planning history.

P.T. Waley (2012), Daniel B. Abraham (2018), and Carola Hein (2018b: 244) corroborate Kusno's standpoint. Hein states that both planners and historians 'have long associated Japanese urban planning to be a practice and a tradition entirely separate from their own'. Waley realizes that failure within the discipline of planning history to inquire the relationship between Japanese and Chinese city development has meant an inability to grasp their convergence and difference re the internationalization of modern planning during the first half of the twentieth century. Such a standpoint is also held by Abraham. He acknowledges that there is still much to know of China's planning history, and how it informs and amalgamates with global histories of urban development and design.

For Abraham (2018), to better understand China's association with planning's internationalization in the past, inquiries must adopt a regional focus. This is because while it is widely recognized that foreign planning models existed in China during the first half of the twentieth century, their implementation varied from province to province. Only after 1949, he claims, were foreign models of planning applied on a truly national level. The early Mao era planners' acceptance of the Soviet model and the nature of statecraft built by the Chinese communists were responsible for the evolution. After 1949 planning systems had more capacity to 'travel' from the regional to national level. Waley (2012) supports Abraham's perspective. He insists the regional scale is the most appropriate starting point to reflect on the many possibilities of convergence between the evolutionary Chinese urban planning system and those existing in foreign lands. He adds, only from better understanding dynamics *within* the Chinese system can the international influence be more accurately evaluated.

If adopting a region-centred approach, and in doing so seeking to reveal Japan's influence on the development of urban places in China, then the northeast of China offers the best entry point. Japan's stamp on the region's urban form was evident after the First Sino-Japanese War (1894–5), for example, in the city of Dalian. From the early 1900s, urban planning and construction under Japanese imperialism took on distinct features in the city. Lui et al. (2020) suggest that Japanese imperialism comprised of four specific phases of urban designing in Dalian. These being 1905–18, 1918–30, 1930–41, and 1941–5. From 1930, comprehensive planning ideas were applied in the city.

The exercising of colonial urban planning by the Japanese was not limited to Dalian or the region of Manchuria (or Manchukuo as it became known following Japan's occupation). It occurred, as noted before, in Taiwan (after 1895) and in Korea (after its annexing in 1910). Taipei and Seoul were, as models of Japanese colonization, subject to Japanese urban environmental reform. However, Japan 'poured the most passion into the construction of Hsinking' (Xu, 2023: 6).

Before discussing urban planning in Hsinking, previously known as Xinjing, brief description of Japan's influence upon Taipei and Seoul's urban design must be given. In Taipei, symbols of Japanese colonial power were expressed through the construction of large-sized public buildings at the urban core and, in Seoul, to make it a 'modern colonial capital' not only were new architectural forms introduced but strategies set up to make urban life cleaner and healthier. In exposing civilizational 'elevation' under the guidance of Japan, in contrast to planning in the motherland, urban designing in the colonial context led to urban cores being wholly refashioned. This reforming of downtowns conveyed Japan's modernist visions for its colonies.

Modern city planning in Japan commences in 1919. In that year the City Planning Act was passed. Yet, in the aftermath of the Great Kanto Earthquake of September 1923, the Special City Planning Act was passed. It gave planners new opportunity to consider large-scale planning application. Records held by the National Archives of Australia, for instance, show the Japanese thirst for grand modern planning ideas pre-1923. In March and April of 1922, a planner employed by the Government of Tokyo, Akira Yanagisawa, visited Sydney, Melbourne, and Canberra. He also met with Australia's leading planning proponent, John Sulman. Although it is unclear if Yanagisawa was directly involved in the composing of the 1930 Tokyo Reconstruction Work scheme, his Australian outing nonetheless demonstrates the Japanese willingness in the years immediately subsequent to the City Planning Act to learn foreign planning models *and* to undertake comprehensive urban planning. The involvement of 'thinking big' and devising grand urban visions was reinforced by the 1930s through imperial ventures. One city, Hsinking, stands out in this regard. More than any other city under Japanese control it defined ultra modernity – 'more modern than the motherland', said Denison and Ren (2017: 105).

In restructuring Hsinking's built environment, in similarity to other urban settlements under Japan colonial authority, new architectural forms were presented. Bill Sewell (2019) describes these design styles as both modern and native. Concerning the 1932 Hsinking city plan, its geometric layout amalgamated idealistic elements. The plan's form 'reflected the Japanese vision of an ideal city and their new role in East Asia' (Guo, 2004: 104), for example, by means of superimposing the new spatial configuration upon the historic Chinese grid layout with its principal north-south axis to symbolize cosmic power. Hsinking's new boulevards, parks, circuses, radial roadways, and buildings denoted stringent Japanese control. However, as impactful as planning was at the urban core, the arranging of building at the urban fringe was also noticeable. In Datong too, American neighbourhood planning theory was used by the Japanese. Naoto Nakajima (2023: 123) describes the 1938 plan for Datong as combining 'the experience of experimental city planning in colonial Manchuria with the academic knowledge of the latest international trends in city planning'. The end result, he alleges, is of historical significance as it lies between the intersection of colonial city planning practice and the academic exploration of city planning. The techniques used by the Japanese in Datong were, Nakajima emphasizes, perceived by the colonizers 'as the most advance tools in modern city planning' (2023: 123).

To expand upon my prior comment regarding the Japanese colonial planning system's integration of foreign ideas and practices, I wish to now highlight that Japanese colonization brought with it Beaux Arts influence. In seeking to apply the most modern planning logic and practices, both consciously and otherwise, Japanese planners employed design conventions allied to Beaux Arts rationality. Furthermore, their logic was imprinted onto the Chinese mind through working in municipal administrations with native persons. Some Chinese administrators, as indicated already, had received their education in Japan. So, against the backdrop of the Japanese remodelling settlements so that an allegedly superior image of local civilization could be built, Chinese officials were able to inform the colonizers of local culture and architectural and spatial traditions but, in alliance, make sense of pre-existing imported foreign planning models given their awareness of urban environmental developments in other parts of the country since the 1920s. Therefore, to summarize, what China's urban planning history highlights is that the country was subject, in different ways in different regions, to both domestic and international dynamics which each imposed what it meant to 'be environmentally modern'. China's planning modernity, in effect, was multi-formed (Denison, 2019). Various planning modernities co-existed.

Following the end of World War Two in 1945, and with the instigation of new governments in Korea and Taiwan, it might be assumed that the Japanese colonial city planning system was abolished. Shun-ichi Watanabe (2016) shows otherwise. He notes that in Korea and Taiwan the pre-1945 system established by the Japanese remained valid, and once Japanese planners returned home there was actually a lack of planning expertise. To know more of the post-war development of planning, he stresses, the requirement is to ask: 'How, and by whom, was this vacuum filled?' (Watanabe, 2016: 17). As a result, from the mid-late 1940s, planning was developed by Chinese persons either educated overseas or at Mainland institutions with curricula based on foreign models. Only by the 1970s, with the revision of laws in Korea and Taiwan, were local planning procedures seen as completely independent from the Japanese colonial planning system. In fact, from the late-1940s to the 1970s, a new wave of Beaux Arts-influenced designing occurred in Taiwan.

5.5 Sino-Western Exchange Pre-1945, and China-Taiwan Exchange Post-1945

U.S.-educated planner Dong Dayou (1936: 359) summarized that he and his peers upon returning to China were 'filled with ambition to create something new and worthwhile'. He remarked that they together formed a new movement, one grounded in doing away 'with poor imitation of Western architecture and to make Chinese architecture truly national'. Evidently, whilst there is much still to learn of China's first generation of modern urban designers, what is known is that upon returning to their homeland it was in the grip of political, educational, and cultural change (Chang, 2017). By the early 1920s, for the first time, a Western-style architectural curriculum was implemented, for example, at Suzhou Industrial Specialised School – and it was replicated at other institutions. Also, a number of publications were freely available. Among such publications was *The Far Eastern Review*, which often published texts referencing architecture, modernism, and nationhood. By the early 1930s, it was joined in the marketplace by publications such as *The Builder* (established in 1932) and *The Chinese Architect* (established in 1933).

Combined with imported publications, written in languages such as English and French, Chinese architects were from the 1930s able to read and publish in a variety of professional-related media. According to Denison and Ren (2008), the situation permitted new discourse to emerge regarding urban beauty, modernity, and architectural meaning, form, and function. Such debate drew attention to contemporary urban designing overseas, which was intensified by organizations such as the Association of Chinese and American Engineers (founded in 1919 with 102 members, 55 of which were American) *and* by the growing numbers of American architects and civil engineers in China from the 1920s. These persons included Jacob Crane (1894–1988), a Chicago planning consultant, who advised Chinese officials (Cody, 1996). Additionally, individuals who attended the Boxer Indemnity Scholarship Program ('the Program') assisted ongoing national construction. The Program enabled young Chinese adults to learn ideas, practices, and ideals instilled by European and American education; such knowledge acquisition was applied in service of China's goals of civilizational progress and material prosperity (Journal of the Association of Chinese and American Engineers, 1920).

As a new phase in Sino-Western exchange, the Program brought Chinese architecture students to live/study in foreign societies. Given the emphasis on the French Beaux Arts in U.S. architecture schools, Chinese students were able to study 'design science' as Paul Cret (1876–1945) at the University of Pennsylvania described it. One such individual who acquired such knowledge was Liang Sicheng (梁思成, 1901–1972), who after education at the previously mentioned academe not only founded Architecture Departments at Northeastern University (in Shenyang in 1928) and Tsinghua University (in Beijing, 1946) but penned the first modern history of Chinese architecture. He, alongside other young Chinese men and women, for example Lin Huiyin (林徽因, 1904–1955), a renowned designer, writer, and heritage advocate, introduced design technologies, practices, and theories hitherto unknown to Chinese society and architectural education.

Of the fifty-five founding members of the Chinese Architects Association, fourteen graduated from University of Pennsylvania, where teachers such as Cret emphasized design principles, authenticity, and 'the modern'. Such logic encouraged architecture graduates, upon returning home, to visit old buildings and 'rediscover' their form and meaning. This occasioned experimentation in China with combining traditional forms with the Western styles seen in U.S. cities/explored as part of higher education. It enabled modernity, in the Chinese setting, to be an opportunity to 'find' buildings with a style and spirit to serve contemporary living. Consequently, thanks to contact with exemplary educators such as Cret, the first generations of overseas-educated Chinese architects were able to not only teach or write with great skill, they were in effect able to influence the subsequent generations of designers in their homeland. Through them, Beaux Arts methods and practices were extended well beyond the American context (Atkin, 2011). Critically too, through new publications such as *The Builder*, the early generations of modern-era Chinese architects and planners practiced with a unified mission. The sense of unified mission was punctuated in *The Builder*'s first edition (in 1932) where the fundamentals of design's value to Chinese society's development were laid bare: architects must work as a community; they must overcome personal interest; they should study in new ways; they should not work in just one place/city; they need to understand their position and mission (Denison and Ren, 2008).

In appreciating the longevity of the Beaux Arts style in East Asia, one must look at Taiwan. When post-1945 the Nationalist government took over the formerly Japanese colonial schools, textbooks and teaching methods were based on Beaux Arts knowledge brought to China in the 1920s by those graduating from Western universities. In the opinion of Fu Chao-Ching (2011), post-1945 programmes of architecture in Taiwan mimicked the curricula of the Central University in Nanjing and the University of Pennsylvania. Owing to architects and teachers leaving China they 'transplanted what they had learned – particularly the *analytique* and the technique of rendering – to architects' offices and schools in Taiwan' (Fu, 2011: 130). The amalgamation of Chinese design traditions with the Beaux Arts pedagogy became so strong that it persisted until the 1980s, for example, culminating with the Chiang Kai-Shek Cultural Complex in Taipei (see Figure 23). The Beaux Arts was, quite simply, 'the best way for Chinese architects in Taiwan to accomplish their goal of achieving a Chinese classical style' (Fu, 2011: 136).

To further explain the longevity of the Beaux Arts in Taiwan the significance of the political context should not be downplayed. In the setting of post-World War Two politics on the island, intense debate existed as to what constituted 'valid' design. Even though a range of different forms of architecture were practised, most were considered 'unsound' for nationally important projects. Taiwan's Nationalist government, established in 1948, sought a design style that represented the spirit of 'new modernity'. Owing to Beaux Arts architecture and traditional Chinese architecture sharing common design principles, for example, symmetry, axis, monumentality, and so on, accordingly, to combine the two styles served to generate an architectural approach that was perceived to 'best express' the dominant political ideology (Denton, 2021; Fu, 2011).

To demonstrate the connection between Taiwanese post-war architecture and the Beaux Arts, Fu (2011) examined the nature of education; he compared the Taiwan Provincial College of Engineering's curriculum in 1955 with the Central University's syllabus (in China) in 1933 and the University of Pennsylvania's in 1918. In doing this 'we can better understand how courses were transmitted from Penn to the Taiwan Provincial College of Engineering, via Mainland China'. Amongst Fu's (2011: 132–133) findings were two

Figure 23 Top: The Chiang Kai-Shek Memorial Hall, and (bottom) The Gate of Great Centrality with the National Theater and National Concert Hall. These buildings, forming the Chiang Kai-Shek Cultural Complex, cover an area of 240,000 square metres in downtown Taipei

Source: The author.

significant suppositions: teachers from China (employed in Taiwan) with a background in Beaux Arts education assumed Western education was better suited to societal needs than traditional Chinese craft-based training; and, the teachers with a Beaux Arts educational background provided their students 'with a first-hand Beaux Arts learning experience'. They, by the 1950s, replaced the traditional grading system with one based on Beaux Arts grading. Similarly, the nature of teaching shifted. Now, in the milieu of Nationalist politics, students in Taiwan learned about the design of triumphal arches and memorial gates. At Taiwan Provincial Cheng Kung University (now known as 國立成功大學 (National Cheng Kung University)), Beaux Arts-type courses were introduced in 1956, and new textbooks were composed. Such developments enabled students to analyse architectural form from fresh standpoints, and to understand notions relating to form, shade, and shadow, that is, basic tenets of Beaux Arts education.

6 Understanding Planning Ideas and Practices from a Global Historical Perspective

The Element has shown that by the early 1900s many countries endeavoured to provide more attractive urban environments for citizens to live and work in. The application of the American City Beautiful planning model encouraged architects and planners to 'think big' so that picturesque, orderly, and dignified settlements could be formed. Technical plans in this pursuit were often accompanied with promotional imagery to communicate the benefits of large-scale urban designing to the public (Shatkin, 2018).

In reviewing the international footprint of the City Beautiful, Anthony Sutcliffe (1981) and Robert Freestone (2007a) highlight the significance of discussions, ideas, and practices concerning aesthetics and environmental aggrandizement. Yet, planning as it evolved in many countries circa 1900–20 dealt with much more than beautification alone. Therefore, to truly understand the international reach of City Beautiful planning requires recognition of its alignment in different localities to considerations of urban efficiency, technocracy, morality, loyalty, citizenship, power, and politics.

According to Stephen Ward (2005: 136), the circumstances of the early 1900s were conducive to the flowering of transnational planning concepts and practices. He notes the changing realities of Western imperialism, professional development within fields such as architecture, and the character of formative planning movements themselves as being fundamental factors that supported the international diffusion of planning ideas and methods: 'In their capacity to transcend national boundaries, these networks, the literature they produced and the discursive events they organised were important media for the creation of a global epistemology of planning which both encouraged and was encouraged by transnational planning practice.'

Christopher Tunnard (1961) notes that to inquire of planning activity in any locality at any time in the past requires four basic questions to be asked: 'Who plans?'; 'What do they plan?'; 'How do their plans reflect particular ideas and values?'; 'In what ways does planning reflect broader societal affairs?' Although the Element has principally focused on grand urban designing in a handful of countries during the early 1900s, it must be recognized that the City Beautiful planning influence transpired in other places, for example, in Panama and New Zealand – see Petrovic (2004), Miller (2007), and Vernon (2020). Similarly, as Arturo Almandoz (2015a: 34) explains, the French urban design heritage that affected urban planning's evolution in the U.S. by the late 1800s also had influence in Latin America. Urban transformation of the type first seen in mid-1800s Paris, Almandoz clarifies (2015a: 36), was adopted in South American capital cities during the late 1800s due to its progressive and civilized symbolism: 'Latin American capitals not only strove to demonstrate their resemblance to the metropolises of the emerging *Belle Époque*, but also tried to manifest their rejection of the *damero* and architectural vocabulary inherited from colonial times.' Indeed, by the commencement of the twentieth century, the process of Haussmann-inspired urban environmental transform-ation was reinforced in some cities by a new wave of comprehensive planning projects. One such example is Buenos Aires, Argentina. In 1906, the domed *Palacio del Congreso de la Nación Argentina* (Palace of the Argentine National Congress) was completed and, by 1910, at the edifice's front, the three-hectare Congress Plaza was laid out. The green space was designed by the Frenchman, Jules Thays (1849–1934) (Figure 24).

South American consciousness of foreign modern planning models expanded as the twentieth century unfolded. However, new attention to overseas urban design systems did not mean that *urbanismo* (urbanism) as it evolved directly corresponded to the practice of monumental urban beautification as seen in contemporary U.S. towns and cities. As to why, the inquiries of Joel Outtes require notice. Outtes (2003) specifies that it was municipal engineers, not architects, who were largely responsible for the design of urban environmental projects by the early 1900s in Latin American countries. In addition, a wide assortment of influences shaped the development of Latin American urban planning systems. In Brazil, for example, whilst Daniel Burnham and Charles Mulford Robinson were taught as part of planning pedagogy by the 1910s, they were typically discussed not as singular leaders but rather in the context of generic planning advancement, that is, alongside European pioneers in past

Figure 24 View of the Palace of the Argentine National Congress from
the Congress Plaza.

Source: The author.

ages. Likewise, in the same decade, South American municipal governments for
the first time sought know-how for better managing urban growth. Said Outtes
(2003: 146): 'This new attitude proved a turning point in the paradigm of
thinking about, and intervening in, cities. It was no longer merely a question
of opening new avenues to improve the circulation of traffic or renewing slum
infested cities centres as in previous cases.'

For every rule, evidently, there are exceptions. Whilst the emergent South
American concept of modern city planning meant it had to be adaptable to the
climate, culture, politics, and traditions of the continent, in São Paulo, Brazil,
the City Beautiful became 'associated with strategies aimed at shaping in spatial
terms the city's identity, as well as the issue of the creation of a new "centre"'
(da Silva Pereira, 2002: 96). Also, in Buenos Aires, grand planning practice still
abounded. In 1924, Jean-Claude Forestier (1861–1930) visited the city, and
some of his Beaux Arts-inspired ideas were integrated into the first Organic
Project by the *Comisión de Estética Edilicia* (Commission of Building
Aesthetic) (Almandoz, 2015b). Forestier, it must be added, between 1925 and
1930, also shaped urban planning in Cuba. In the capital city of Havana, with the
backing of President Gerardo Machado (1871–1939), he designed numerous

parks (Hartman, 2019a). In 1926 he also presented the Havana City Project with its network of axial boulevards and substantial green spaces; the plan thus referenced environmental features aligned to Cuba's past and present, that is, the 'Spanish', the French', the 'American', and the 'Cuban' (Hartman, 2019b). Moreover, in the 1920s, observes Susana Torre (2002: 550), design education in Latin America changed. With growing focus upon regional histories, schools of architecture sought to devise curricula that explored and explained the role of aesthetics and environmental design to national identity from shared colonial heritage. By the 1940s educations systems 'began extricating themselves from both their Beaux-Arts and engineering school traditions'.

6.1 Comprehending the City Beautiful in a Transnational Framework

It is believed by innumerable historians that inquiries of past life, where possible, should reinvent knowledge. Remarks Akira Iriye (2007), historians have an obligation to not only illuminate past events via the use of empirical evidence, they also have a responsibility to offer alternative explanations and devise new conceptual frameworks in order to show what happened in the past and why. As I indicate in Section 1 of the Element, the discipline of Global History offers an intellectual platform to re-evaluate the diffusion of urban planning ideas and practices. Certainly, as presented in the Element from Section 2 onwards, the importation of City Beautiful planning into many countries reveals their 'connected history' to the U.S. Given its international footprint, in effect, the City Beautiful belonged to more than just its home nation of the United States.

Despite acknowledged flaws, the discipline of Planning History has in recent decades highlighted the international qualities of modern urban planning (Ward, Freestone, and Silver, 2011). Studies have underscored that during the late 1800s and early 1900s great leaps forward in planning thinking and practice occurred. The inquiries have shown that with the establishing of international contacts, an 'epistemic community' was formed. It is described by Peter Haas (1992: 3) as 'a network of professional with recognized expertise and competence in a particular domain and an authoritative claim to policy-relevant knowledge within that domain or issue-area'.

Stephen Ward (2002 and 2005) has explained that transnational planning practices grew from about 1900: central to their internationalization was the organizing of conferences, exhibitions, and design competitions; the establishing of planning schools; and, the publishing of materials on planning theory and practice. Collectively these matters, he says, 'helped promote planning innovation and diffusion and played key roles in establishing an increasingly common international repertoire from which theories and techniques could, in various combinations, be drawn' (Ward, 2005: 121). But, of note too, there was 'certainly no complete homogeneity in the way this repertoire was synthesised and used by all planners in all countries' (Ward, 2005: 121). As such, attention to the role and significance of urban environmental embellishment within the development of national planning systems varied from country to country, and from planner to planner too.

Anthony Sutcliffe (1981) has clarified that planning movements within nations during the early 1900s were basically never more than an assembly of individuals. However, he has also identified that different 'personalities' of planners existed at that time. These dispositions, he shows, affected the capacity of a foreign planning exemplar to have presence and influence within a nation's planning system. Hence, in Sutcliffe's view, when a nation had 'cosmopolitan planners' and 'intermediary planners', then the appeal of a foreign planning model could help override existing national ones. Yet this alone did not allow for the widespread 'take-up' of a foreign urban design model. For a planning paradigm to have profound imprint, it was necessary, adds Sutcliffe, for domestic contexts to be favourable; for example, the elites need to be willing to change the political-legal instruments of planning.

To further explain the appeal of a foreign planning model, scholars such as Sutcliffe, Ward, Rodgers, Stapleton, Stetler, and Freestone have identified the critical role of two-way flows of ideas and practices, that is, as what happened between the U.S and France during the late 1800s and early 1900s. In the home of the Beaux Arts, France, its planning narrative by the first decade of the twentieth century was affected by urban designing advancement in the U.S.; the City Beautiful offered a lesson in civic improvement for the French. However, Chicago-type planning schemes were not implemented in France. As the Element highlights, the take-up of the City Beautiful planning model in its most blown-up form, that is, large-scale urban planning, was evident in some countries but, in contrast, was too ambitious and/or irrelevant for many other places. Sutcliffe (1981) noticed the French were unimpressed by the American take on Beaux Arts principles and aesthetics, and in Britain, by way of offering another example, the breadth of City Beautiful impact was hindered by the nature of the 1909 Housing, Town Planning, Etc. Act. Burnham-esque plans were, quite simply, too costly to be seriously considered by most municipal governments.

Although the Element has concentrated upon large-sized City Beautiful planning schemes, it has been mentioned, for example, in Sections 3 and 4, that watered-down versions existed with regard to the laying out of urban cores and public spaces in the Philippines and Australia. These two countries were by no means unique; in the U.S., and in other countries, small-sized City Beautiful schemes were composed. Jon Peterson (1976) shows that smaller-scale concerns led to the planning model's application throughout the U.S.; not all towns and cities had an intention to implement comprehensive urban plans. So, to reference Ward's earlier remark of the rising global interest in planning circa 1900, it is important to recognize that City Beautiful thinking and practice was adapted to suit local conditions and local needs. In the case of its importation into foreign lands such as Australia and New Zealand, it was adapted to meet not only local conditions and needs but local customs too (Freestone, 2023).

Akira Iriye (2004) and Ian Tyrrell (2009) note that the transnational study of history encourages both exploration and explanation of the contacts and connections between countries. Such attention to the transmission of planning ideas has been investigated and explained by individuals referenced in the Element. Their inquiries and conclusions have opened windows for supplementary analysis of the American City Beautiful's propagation to foreign lands. Each scholar, in different ways, and with attention to different topics, contexts, and places, has exposed why City Beautiful planning occurred beyond the territorial borders of the U.S. What they have also collectively shown, first, is that the City Beautiful was able to diffuse to some foreign localities given the U.S.' capacity to 'exchange' power. In the Philippines, as an example, the City Beautiful had impact because the island chain was from 1898 to 1946 under American political authority. In contrast, the U.S. had no direct power over goings-on in, say, China. Influence there emanated from individuals and private companies. So, with a less robust type of 'exchange', the City Beautiful planning model was not able to establish itself in such a profound manner as it did in the Philippine Islands. Second, the sustainability of the City Beautiful was shaped by not just who imported it but by who then took it up. In the Philippines a key agent in this regard was the Filipinos employed by the Bureau of Public Works. They adapted the City Beautiful model in the frame of decolonization to both beautify and 'nativize' urban fabrics. As an upshot, the planning model was still in use long after American planners had left the country *and* after its use had waned in North America.

The *Cambridge Elements in Global Urban History* book series, in placing new attention upon transnational analysis, thereby contributes to the manufacture of a new type of historical intelligence. The generic approach of the book series encourages the realization that, as a case in point, an urban planning model traditionally viewed as 'belonging' to one nation can in fact be decentred. Given that the Element recontextualizes the City Beautiful, it does not deconstruct U.S. History. More exactly, by placing the City Beautiful into a global context supplements existing knowledge of the U.S. and its connections during the late 1800s and early 1900s to the wider world.

As much as the City Beautiful had influence upon certain nations' urban planning system's evolution, in many parts of the world its imprint was at best negligible. As to why, the answer might lie in how planning knowledge flows are evaluated and filtered. In consequence, what constitutes 'good planning' in one place is judged as 'bad planning' in another. As a result, one planning model may be deemed unfitting, whereas another more befitting for 'naturalization'. However, as Stephen Ward (2018) broadly explains, the process of the importation and exportation of planning ideas and practices varies. Thus, a typology of diffusion can assist in explaining how the City Beautiful was sent overseas to some places, but, at the same time, to not all foreign lands. The typology, Ward notes, exposes two basic matters. First, a planning model's *imposition* – by authority or contest or negotiation – and, second, its *borrowing* – undiluted, selective, and synthetic. Put succinctly, Ward (2018: 85) shows that human agency in the receiving country 'has the greatest importance in types of borrowing', and structure makes its biggest impact 'where exogenous planning arrives by imposition, ostensibly suppressing all indigenous agency in its most authoritarian variant'.

The *Cambridge Elements in Global Urban History* book series, to restate an earlier point, offers new windows from which to (re)evaluate the internationalization of urban historical phenomenon. The book series grants new platforms from which to generate dialogue about civilizations and the urban environmental forms they produced. In this intellectual setting there is fresh opportunity to rethink the importance of the American City Beautiful. It also offers new occasion to think about why its adoption was met with vacillation and/or resistance in some countries. In the case of Canada, Gilbert Stelter (2000: 105) remarks that whilst some planners devised City Beautiful schemes, others were simply unenthralled by the American model of urban design. Similarly in Mexico, government officials shied away from the comprehensive plans for formal civic centres in vogue in the U.S. (McMichael Reese, 2002). Also, in Japan, Western planning ideas inspired new interest in garden cities and housing layouts, but not the redesign of urban cores (Sorensen, 2002).

Notwithstanding the examples of hesitation, the international success of the City Beautiful is hard to deny. The rise and spread of City Beautiful planning, among other things, accentuates the importance of civic activism in instigating urban reform. Evidently, with the growth of the City Beautiful so too did derivatives of 'Grand Manner' planning emerge: for example, in 1930s Ankara, Türkiye, in New Delhi, India due to Edwin Lutyens (1869–1944); in Berlin, Germany, with Albert Speer's (1905–1981) 1937–42 city plan; and in

Figure 25 Top: The vista along Kartavya Path (formerly Rajpath) to Rashtrapati Bhavan (formerly known as the Viceroy's House). Bottom: Monumental city planning alongside the use of modern architectural forms. A view of the *Eixo Monumental* (Monumental Axis) to the *Congresso Nacional* (National Congress) in Brasilia.

Source: The author.

Addis Ababa, Ethiopia, with Ignazio Guidi's and Cesare Valle's late-1930s/ early-1940s plans as part of Italy's colonial occupation. At the same time, monumental examples of city planning occurred post-World War Two, for example, in Brasilia, Brazil (see Figure 25). Whilst it is apparent that the legacy of the City Beautiful was mixed from country to country, its achievements were nonetheless considerable and its ideals garnered the attention of planners who intended to re-establish order and beauty within built fabrics. Significantly as well, today's notion of urban beauty and order, akin to ideas of environmental attractiveness held decades ago by City Beautiful advocates, draws upon historical precedents (Hall, 1997; Macdonald, 2012). As a subfield of urban planning, physical beauty *is still seen* as vital to place-making, imageability, and public well-being.

For the purpose of précis, there is still much to learn about the urban past and the design of built fabrics (Nightingale, 2018). Likewise, there will always be the need to improve and reexamine our understanding of what is already known. In terms of past planning ideas and practices, there is still an assortment of planning histories to investigate within both national and international settings. With the narrative of the City Beautiful traditionally centring itself upon 'great plans', 'great planners', and the U.S., it is imperative now to realize that the City Beautiful application occurred in many different countries *and* was done so often by individuals of lesser vocational stature. In view of this historical fact, existing written history must be challenged. The proponents of the City Beautiful, particularly those outside the West, are presently neglected voices within the global historiography of urban design. They need to be brought forward. This will not only reduce the need to rely upon the existent 'great plans and great planners' narrative; it will also build new canons to reshape our understanding of urban communities' past character. In turn, expanded urban historical knowledge can affect the nature of heritage strategies in towns and cities scattered throughout the world, that is, in those places touched by City Beautiful planning.

References

Unknown author (1898) The Architecture of Our Large Provincial Towns – Dundee. *The Builder* 74, 139–146.

Unknown author (1910) Town Planning Conference, London, 1910. *Art and Progress* 1(7), 206.

Unknown author (1913) Dundee Central Improvements. *The Town Planning Review* 4(2), 177.

Unknown author (1915a) Illustrations: Libraries, Dundee. *The Builder* 108, 585.

Unknown author (1915b) Central Improvement Scheme, Dundee. *The Builder* 109, 31.

Unknown author (1920) Introduction. *Journal of the Association of Chinese and American Engineers* 1, 1–3.

Unknown author (1927) Canton Adopts New 'City Plan'. *The New York Times*, March 13, 13.

Unknown author (1929a) Proposed Plan for Nanking, China's National Metropolis. Mr Lu Yen Chih's Last Piece of Work. *Liangyou Pictorial* 40, 3.

Unknown author (1929b) The Proposed Plan for the Buildings of the Five Yuan of the National Government (Work of Late Mr Lu). *Liangyou Pictorial* 40, 3.

Unknown author (1930) Planning the New Chinese National Capital. *The Chinese Social and Political Science Review* 14, 372–382.

Unknown author (1930) Greater Shanghai: Building a New Port and City. *The Far Eastern Review* 26(6), 296–297.

Unknown author (1931a) Building a New Shanghai. *The Far Eastern Review* 27(6), 348–351.

Unknown author (1931b) Canton – A World Port. *The Far Eastern Review* 27(6), 352–358.

Unknown author (1933) Civic Centre of the Greater Shanghai Plan. *Shanghai Youth* 33(21), 1–3.

Unknown author (1934) Plan of the Administrative Area in the Centre of the Greater Shanghai Municipality. *The Chinese Architect* 2(9–10), 24–27.

Unknown author (2024) Canberra, the Seat of Government. In *National Capital Authority: A Place for All Australians* [online] www.nca.gov.au/education/canberras-history/canberra-seat-government#.

Abercrombie, P. (1910) The Plan for Chicago. *The Town Planning Review* 1(1), 56–65.

Abraham, D. T. (2018) The Use of Planning History in China. In C. Hein, ed., *The Routledge Handbook of Planning History*. London: Routledge, 260–272.

Adams, T. (1936) *Outline of Town and City Planning: A Review of Past Efforts and Modern Aims*. New York: Russell Sage.

Adas, M. (2014) *Machines as a Measure of Man: Science, Technology, and Ideologies of Western Dominance*. Ithaca: Cornell University Press.

Adshead, S. (1910) Cathays Park, Cardiff. *The Town Planning Review* 1(2), 148–150.

Adshead, S. (1914) The Democratic View of Town Planning. *The Town Planning Review* 5(3), 183–194.

Allan, C. M. (1965) The genesis of British Urban Redevelopment with Special Reference to Glasgow. *The Economic History Review* 18(3), 598–613.

Almandoz, A. (2015a) Urbanization and Urbanism in Latin America: From Haussmann to CIAM. In A. Almandoz, ed., *Planning Latin America's Capital Cities 1850–1950*. London: Routledge, 13–44.

Almandoz, A. (2015b) *Modernization, Urbanization and Development in Latin America, 1900s–2000s*. London: Routledge.

Atkin, T. (2011) Chinese Architecture Students at the University of Pennsylvania in the 1920s. In J. Cody, N. Steinhardt, and T. Akin, eds., *Chinese Architecture and the Beaux Arts*. Honolulu: University of Hawai'i Press, 45–72.

Bennett, E. (1917) Public Buildings and Quasi-Public Buildings. In J. Nolen, ed., *City Planning. A Series of Papers Presenting the Essential Elements of a City Plan*. New York: D. Appleton, 103–116.

Best, J. (2009) Empire Builders: American City Planning in the Philippines. *Bulletin of the American Historical Collection* 37(2), 25–34.

Boyce, W. D. (1914) The Philippine Islands. Chicago: Rand McNally.

Boyer, C. (1983) *Dreaming the Rational City: The Myth of American City Planning*. Cambridge, MA: MIT Press.

Brain, D. (1989) Discipline and Style: The Ecole des Beaux-Arts and the Social Production of an American Architecture. *Theory and Society* 18, 807–868.

Brody, D. (2010) *Visualizing American Empire: Orientalism and Imperialism in the Philippines*. Chicago: University of Chicago Press.

Brown, N. (2014) *A History of Canberra*. Melbourne: Cambridge University Press.

Burnham, D. H. (1911a) The Banquet. In Royal Institute of British Architects, ed., *Town Planning Conference. London 10th–15th October 1910. Transactions*. London: Royal Institute of British Architects, 92–108.

Burnham, D. H. (1911b) A City of the Future under a Democratic Government. In Royal Institute of British Architects, ed., *Town Planning Conference.*

London 10th–15th October 1910. Transactions. London: Royal Institute of British Architects, 368–378.

Burnham, D. H. and Bennett, E. (1905) *Report on a Plan for San Francisco*. San Francisco: Sunset Press.

Burnham, D. H. and Anderson, P. (1906) Report on Improvements at Manila. In *Report of the Philippine Commission, Part 1*. Washington, DC: The Government Printing Office, 627–635.

Burnham, D. H. and Bennett, E. (1909) *Plan of Chicago*. Chicago: The Commercial Club.

Cameron, H. F. (1914) Provincial Centers in the Philippine Islands. *Quarterly Bulletin, Bureau of Public Works* 2(4), 3–11.

Carroll, P. (2011) The Beaux Arts in Another Register: Governmental Administrative and Civic Centers in City Plans of the Republican Era. In J. Cody, N. Steinhardt, and T. Akin, eds., *Chinese Architecture and the Beaux Arts*. Honolulu: University of Hawai'i Press, 315–332.

Casteñeda Anastacio, L. (2016) *The Foundations of the Modern Philippine State*. New York: Cambridge University Press.

Chang, C.-W. (2017) A Ground between Beaux-Arts Modernism, and Chineseness: Tracing Modernities in China's Architectural Education and Practice, 1919–1949. *Charette* 4(2), 59–71.

Cherry, G. E. (1974) *The Evolution of British Town Planning*. Leighton Buzzard: Leonard Hill Books.

Cherry, G. E., Jordan, H., and Kafkoula, K. (1993) Gardens, Civic Art and Town Planning: The Work of Thomas H. Mawson (1861–1933). *Planning Perspectives* 8(3), 307–332.

Churchward, L. G. (1972) *Australia and America 1788–1972*. An Alternative History. Sydney: APCOL.

Clark, K. (2011) *Moscow: The Fourth Rome*. Cambridge, MA: Harvard University Press.

Cody, J. (1996) American Planning in Republican China, 1911–1937. *Planning Perspectives* 11(4), 339–377.

Cody, J. (2001) *Building in China: Henry K. Murphy's 'Adaptive Architecture' 1914–1935*. Hong Kong: Chinese University of Hong Kong Press.

Cody, J. (2003) *Exporting American Architecture, 1870–2000*. London: Routledge.

Commission of Fine Arts (1923) *The Plan of the National Capital: 9th Report of the Commission of Fine Arts*. Washington, DC: Government Printing Office.

Crawford, C. E. (2022) *Spatial Revolution: Architecture and Planning in the Early Soviet Union*. Ithaca: Cornell University Press.

Crisostomo, I. T. (1971) *Quezon City: Ang Paglikha ng Inyong Lungsod*. Quezon City: Capital Publishing House.

Croly, H. (1906) The Promised City of San Francisco. *The Architectural Record* 19(6), 425–436.

Crossette, B. (1999) *The Great Hill Stations of Asia*. Boulder: Basic Books.

da Silva Pereira, M. (2002) The Time of the Capitals: Rio de Janeiro and São Pualo. In A. Almandoz, ed., *Planning Latin America's Capital Cities*. London: Routledge, 75–108.

Dakudao, M. (1994) The Imperial Consulting Architect: Willia, E. Parsons (1872–1939). *Bulletin of the American Historical Collection* 22(1), 7–43.

Denison, E. (2019) Trans-Colonial Modernities in East Asia. *Proceedings of the Connected Histories, Cosmopolitan Cities: Towards Inter-Imperial and Trans-Colonial Historian of Cities in Asia, 1800–1960*. Singapore: National University of Singapore, 1–22.

Denison, E. and Ren, G. Y. (2008) *Modernism in China: Architectural Visions and Revolutions*. Chichester: John Wiley and Sons.

Denison, E. and Ren, G. Y. (2017) *Ultra-Modernism: Architecture and Modernity in Manchuria*. Hong Kong: Hong Kong University Press.

Denton, K. A. (2021) *The Landscape of Historical Memory*. Hong Kong: Hong Kong University Press.

Doane, R. H. (1918) Architecture in the Philippines. *Quarterly Bulletin: Bureau of Public Works* 7(2), 2–7.

Doon, D. [Dong, D.] (1935) Greater Shanghai – Greater Vision. *The China Critic* 10(5), 104–107.

Doon, D. [Dong, D.] (1936) Architecture Chronicle. *T' ien Hsia Monthly* 3(4), 358–362.

Draper, J. (1982) *Edward H. Bennett: Architect and City Planning, 1874–1954*. Chicago: The Art Institute of Chicago.

Esherick, J. W. (1999) *Remaking the Chinese City: Modernity and National Identity, 1900–1950*. Honolulu: University of Hawai'i Press.

Fischer, K. F. (1989) Canberra: Myths and Models. *The Town Planning Review* 60(2), 155–194.

Freeman, J. C. (1975) Thomas Mawson: Imperial Missionary of British Town-Planning. *RACAR: Revue c' Art Canadienne/Canadian Art Review* 2(2), 37–47.

Freeman, J. M. (1990) *W.D. Caröe: His Architectural Achievements*. Manchester: Manchester University Press.

Freestone, R. (1998) The City Beautiful: Towards an Understanding of the Australian Experience. *Journal of Architectural and Planning Research* 15(2), 91–108.

Freestone, R. (2007a) The Internationalization of the City Beautiful. *International Planning Studies* 12(1), 21–34.

Freestone, R. (2007b) *Designing Australia's Cities: Culture, Commerce and the City Beautiful, 1900–1930.* Sydney: University of New South Wales Press.

Freestone, R. (2010) *Urban Nation: Australian Planning Heritage.* Collingwood: Csiro.

Freestone, R. (2023) City Beautiful Movement. In *Oxford Bibliographies in Urban Studies* [online] www.oxfordbibliographies.com/display/document/obo-9780190922481/obo-9780190922481-0069.xml.

Fu, C.-C. (2011) Beaux Arts Practice and Education by Chinese Architects in Taiwan. In J. Cody, N. Steinhardt, and T. Akin, eds., *Chinese Architecture and the Beaux Arts.* Honolulu: University of Hawai'i Press, 127–143.

Gordon, D. (2018) Politics, Power, and Urban Form. In C. Hein, ed., *The Routledge Handbook of Planning History.* London: Routledge, 301–312.

Gournay, I. and Crosnier, L. (2013) American Architecture Students in Belle Epoque Paris: Scholastic Strategies and Achievements at the Ecole des Beux-Arts. *The Journal of the Gilded Age and Progressive Era* 12(2), 154–198.

Griffin, W. B. (1913) Canberra: An Architectural and Developmental Possibilities of Australia's Capital City. *Building* (November) 13(75), 65–72.

Guo, Q. (2004) Changchun: Unfinished Capital Planning in Manzhouguo, 1932–42. *Urban History* 31(1), 100–117.

Haas, J. (2019) *The San Francisco Civic Center: A History of the Design, Controversies and Realization of a City Beautiful Masterpiece.* Reno: The University of Nevada Press.

Haas, P. (1992) Introduction: Epistemic Communities and International Policy Coordination. *International Organization* 46(1), 1–35.

Hall, T. (1997) *Planning Europe's Capital Cities: Aspects of Nineteenth Century Urban Development.* London: Routledge.

Hartman, J. (2019a) Silent Witnesses: Modernity, Colonialism, and Jean-Claude Forestier's Unfinished Plans for Havana. *Journal of the Society of Architectural Historians* 78(3), 292–311.

Hartman, J. (2019b) *Dictator's Dreamscape: How Architecture and Vision Built Machado's Cuba and Invented Modern Havana.* Pittsburgh: University of Pittsburgh Press.

Headon, D. (2003) *The Symbolic Role of the National Capital: From Colonial Argument to 21st Century Ideals.* Canberra: National Capital Authority.

Hein, C. (2018a) The What, Why, and How of Planning History. In C. Hein, ed., *The Routledge Handbook of Planning History.* London: Routledge, 1–10.

Hein, C. (2018b) Idioms of Japanese Planning Historiography. In C. Hein, ed., *The Routledge Handbook of Planning History.* London: Routledge, 244–259.

Hilling, J. (1976) *The Historic Architecture of Wales: An Introduction*. Cardiff: Cardiff University Press.

Hines, T. S. (1972) The Imperial Façade: Daniel H. Burnham and American Architectural Planning in the Philippines. *Pacific Historical Review* 41(1), 33–53.

Hines, T. S. (1973) American Modernism in the Philippines: The Forgotten Architecture of William E. Parsons. *Journal of the Society of Architectural Historians* 32(4), 316–326.

Hines, T. S. (2009) *Burnham of Chicago: Architect and Planner*. Chicago: University of Chicago Press.

Hirata, K. (2023) Moa's Steeltown: Industrial City, Colonial Legacies, and Local Political Economy in Early Communist China. *Journal of Urban History* 49(1), 85–110.

Howe, F. (1905) *The City: The Hope of Democracy*. New York: Charles Scribner's Sons.

Immerwahr, D. (2021) The Iron Hand of Power: US Architectural Imperialism in the Philippines. *Architecture History* 64, 163–186.

Iriye, A. (2004) Transnational History. *Contemporary European History* 13(2), 211–222.

Iriye, A. (2007) The Transnational Turn. *Diplomatic History* 31(3), 373–376.

Jackson, F. (1895) *Jackson's Famous Pictures of the World's Fair*. Chicago: White City Art.

Kahn, J. (1979) *Imperial San Francisco: Politics and Planning in an Americana City, 1897–1906*. Lincoln: University of Nebraska Press.

Kirsch, S. (2017) Aesthetic Regime Change: The Burnham Plan and US Landscape Imperialism in the Philippines. *Philippine Studies: Historical and Ethnographical Viewpoints* 65(3), 315–356.

Klassen, W. (2010) *Architecture in the Philippines: Filipino Building in a Cross-Cultural Context*. Cebu City: University of San Carlos Press.

Kramer, P. (2006) *The Blood of Government: Race, Empire, the United States and the Philippines*. Chapel Hill: University of North Carolina Press.

Kuan, S. (2011) Between Beaux Arts and Modernism: Dong Dayou and the Architecture of 1930s Shanghai. In J. Cody, N. Steinhardt, and T. Akin, eds., *Chinese Architecture and the Beaux Arts*. Honolulu: University of Hawai'i Press, 169–192.

Kusno, A. (2018) Southeast Asia. In C. Hein, ed., *The Routledge Handbook of Planning History*. London: Routledge, 218–229.

Lamb, C. R. (1898) Civic Architecture from its Constructive Side. *Municipal Affairs: A Quarterly Magazine Devoted to the Consideration of City Problems from the Standpoint of the Taxpayer and Citizen* 2(1), 46–72.

Li, H. (2018) *Building for Oil: Daqing and the Formation of the Chinese Socialist State*. Cambridge, MA: Harvard University Asia Center.

Li, II. (2022) Soviet Specialist's Urban Planning Technical Assistance to China, 1949–1959. *Planning Perspectives* 37(4), 815–839.

Lincoln, T. (2021) *An Urban History of China*. Cambridge: Cambridge University Press.

Liu, Y., Dupre, K., Jin, X., and Weaver, D. (2020) Dalian's Unique Planning History and Its Contested Heritage in Urban Regeneration. *Planning Perspectives* 35(5), 873–894.

Lu, Y. C. (1929a) Memorials to Dr Sun Yat-sen in Nanking and Canton. *The Far Eastern Review* 27(6), 97–101.

Lu, Y. C. (1929b) *Draft Outline for the Capital Metropolitan Area*. Nanjing: Secretariat of the Capital Construction Commission.

Macdonald, E. (2012) Beauty. In R. Weber and R. Crane, eds., *The Oxford Handbook of Urban Planning*. Oxford: Oxford University Press, 105–119.

Malcolm, G. (1916) *The Government of the Philippine Islands: Its Development and Fundamentals*. New York: The Lawyer's Co-Operative.

Mawson, T. (1911) *Civic Art: Studies in Town Planning, Parks, Boulevards, and Open Spaces*. London: B.T. Batsford.

Mawson, T. (1914) *The City of Calgary: Past, Present and Future*. London: B. T. Batsford and Sons.

McMichael Reese, C. (2002) The Urban Development of Mexico City, 1850–1930. In A. Almandoz, ed., *Planning Latin America's Capital Cities 1850–1950*. London: Routledge, 139–169.

Meyer, J. F. (1978) 'Feng Shui' of the Chinese City. *History of Religions* 18(2), 138–155.

Miller, C. (2007) The City Beautiful in New Zealand. In C. Miller and M. Roche, eds., *Heritage and Planning History: Case Studies from the Pacific Rim*. Newcastle: Cambridge Scholars, 8–32.

Miller, S. (1984) *Benevolent Assimilation: The American Conquest of the Philippines, 1899–1903*. New Haven: Yale University Press.

Moore, C. (1902) *The Improvement of the Park System of the District of Columbia*. Washington, DC: Government Printing Office.

Moore, C. (1921a) *Daniel H. Burnham: Architect Planner of Cities Vol. 1*. Boston: Houghton Mifflin.

Moore, C. (1921b) *Daniel H. Burnham. Architect Planner of Cities Vol. 2*. Boston: Houghton Mifflin.

Morley, I. (2007) The City Beautiful Movement. In D. Goldfield, ed., *Encyclopedia of American Urban History Vol. 1*. Thousand Oaks: Sage, 150–152.

Morley, I. (2009) Representing a City and Nation: Wales' Matchless Civic Centre. The *Welsh History Review* 24(3), 56–81.

Morley, I. (2013) Philippine Connections: Canberra's Plan and Nationhood. *Fabrications. The Journal of the Society of Architectural Historians, Australia and New Zealand* 23(1), 26–57.

Morley, I. (2018a) *Cities and Nationhood: American Imperialism and Urban Design in the Philippines, 1898–1916.* Honolulu: University of Hawai'i Press.

Morley, I. (2018b) The First Filipino City Beautiful Plans. *Planning Perspectives* 33(3), 433–447.

Morley, I. (2018c) The Filipinization of the American City Beautiful, 1916–1935. *Journal of Planning History* 17(4), 251–280.

Morley, I. (2019) *American Colonisation and the City Beautiful: Filipinos and Planning in the Philippines. 1916–35.* London: Routledge.

Morley, I. (2021) Spatial Change and the Cholera Epidemic in Manila. In M. Gharipour and C. DeClerq, eds., *Epidemic Urbanism: Contagious Disease in Global Cities.* Chicago: Intellect, 289–295.

Morley, I. (2023) *Remodelling to Prepare for Independence: The Philippine Commonwealth, Decolonisation, Cities and Public Works, c. 1935–46.* London: Routledge.

Morley, I. (2024) The Pensionados Program Architects Return Home. *Journal of the Society of Architectural Historians* 83(1), 15–17.

Mumford, L. (1961) *The City in History.* New York: Harcourt, Inc.

Musgrove, C. (2013) *China's Contested Capital: Architecture, Ritual, and Response in Nanjing.* Hong Kong: Hong Kong University Press.

Nakajima, N. (2023) The Datong City Plan (1938): The Three Week-Process of Organizing Planning Ideas and Techniques towards the Construction of a New Urban Area under Japanese Occupation. *Planning Perspectives* 38(1), 99–125.

New South Wales Government (1909) *Report of the Royal Commission for the Improvement of the City of Sydney and its Suburbs.* Sydney: W.A. Gullick, Government Printer.

Nightingale, C. (2018) The Global Urban History Project. *Planning Perspectives* 33(1), 135–138.

O' Connell, L. M. (2020) Ecole des Beaux Arts. In *Oxford Bibliographies in Urban Studies* [online] www.oxfordbibliographies.com/display/document/obo-9780190922467/obo-9780190922467-0016.xml.

Osborn, R. J. and Reiner, T. A. (1962) Soviet City Planning: Current Issues and Future Perspectives. *Journal of the American Institute of Planners* 28(4), 239–250.

Outtes, J. (2003) Developing Society through the City: The Gensis of City Planning in Brazil and Argentina (1894–1945). *Bulletin of Latin American Research* 22(2), 137–164.

Pante, M. (2019) *A Capital City at the Margins: Quezon City and Urbanization in the Twentieth-Century Philippines.* Quezon City: Ateneo de Manila University Press.

Parsons, W. E. (1915) Burnham as a Pioneer of City Planning. *The Architectural Record* 38, 13–31.

Pegrum, R. (2008) *The Bush Capital: How Australia Chose Canberra as Its Federal Capital.* Boorowa: The Watermark Press.

Perks, W. T. (1985) Idealism, Orchestration and Science in Early Canadian Planning: Calgary and Vancouver Re-Visited, 1914/1928. *Environments* 17(2), 1–28.

Peterson, J. (1976) The City Beautiful Movement: Forgotten Origins and Lost Meanings. *Journal of Urban History* 2(4), 415–434.

Peterson, J. (2003) *The Birth of City Planning in the United States, 1840–1917.* Baltimore: The John Hopkins University Press.

Petrovic, E. (2004) Early Twentieth Century Town Planning Improvements in New Zealand. *AHA: Architectural History Aotearoa* 1, 71–81.

Prudente Sta. Maria, F. (2010) In the Steps of the Founder. In P. G. Alcazaren, I. Cruz, F. Prudente Sta. Maria, M. Quezon III, and R. Samson, eds., *Quezon City: The Rise of Asia's City of the Future.* Quezon City: Studio 5 Designs, 47–87.

Rebori, A. N. (1917a) The Work of William E. Parsons in the Philippine Islands. Part 1. *The Architectural Record* 41, 305–324.

Rebori, A. N. (1917b) The Work of William E. Parsons in the Philippine Islands. Part 2. *The Architectural Record* 41, 423–434.

Reed, R. R. (1976) *City of Pines: The Origins of Baguio as a Colonial Hill Station and Colonial Capital.* Berkeley: Center for South and Southeast Asia Studies.

Reid, P. (2002) *Canberra Following Griffin.* Canberra: National Archives of Australia.

Reps, J. (1965) *The Making of Urban America: A History of City Planning in the United States.* Princeton: Princeton University Press.

Reps, J. (1983) Burnham before Chicago: The Birth of Modern American City Planning. *Art Institute of Chicago Museum Studies* 10 (The Art Institute of Chicago Centennial Lectures), 190–217.

Reps, J. (1997) *Canberra 1912.* Melbourne: Melbourne University Press.

Robinson, C. M. (1901) *The Improvement of Towns and Cities.* New York: The Knickerbocker Press.

Robinson, C. M. (1904) *Modern Civic Art, or, the City Made Beautiful.* New York: G.P. Putnam's Sons.

Rodgers, D. T. (1998) *Atlantic Crossings: Social Politics in a Progressive Age.* Cambridge: The Belknap Press of Harvard University Press.

Sandoval-Strausz, A. K. and Kwak, N. H. (2018) Why Transnational Urban History? In A. K. Sandavol-Strausz and N. H. Kwak, eds., *Making Cities Global: The Transnational Turn in Urban History.* Philadelphia: University of Philadelphia Press, 1–13.

Schaffer, K. (2003) *Daniel H. Burnham: Visionary Architect and Planning.* New York: Rizzoli.

Schubert, D. and Sutcliffe, A. (1996) The 'Haussmannization' of London? The Planning and Construction of Kingsway-Aldwych, 1889–1935. *Planning Perspectives* 11(2), 115–144.

Sewell, B. (2019) *Constructing Empire. The Japanese in Changchun, 1905–45.* Vancouver: University of British Columbia Press.

Shatkin, A. (2018) The Visual Culture of Planning. *Journal of Planning History* 17(3), 300–319.

Shen, Y. (1933) Downtown Area Development Plan (市中心區域建設計劃). *Shanghai Youth* 33(21), 1–5.

Simon, M. (1996) The Beaux-Arts Atelier in America. In J. Kinnard and K. Schwartz, eds., *84ᵗʰ ACSA Annual Meeting and Technology Conference Proceedings* [online] www.acsa-arch.org/proceedings/Annual%20Meeting%20Proceedings/ACSA.AM.84/ACSA.AM.84.76.pdf.

Sit, V. (1996) Soviet Influence on Urban Planning in Beijing, 1949–1991. *Town Planning Review* 67(4), 457–484.

Smith, C. (1994) *Urban Disorder and the Shape of Belief: The Great Chicago Fire, the Haymarket Bomb, and the Model Town of Pullman.* Chicago: University of Chicago Press.

Smith, C. (2006) *The Plan of Chicago.* Chicago: University of Chicago Press.

Sonne, W. (2004) *Representing the State: Capital City Planning in the Early Twentieth-Century.* Munich: Prestel.

Sorensen, A. (2002) *The Making of Urban Japan.* London: Routledge.

Stapleton, K. (2007) Warfare and Modern Urban Administration. In D. Strand and S. Cochran, eds., *Cities in Motion. Interior, Coast, and Diaspora in Transnational China.* Berkeley: Institute of East Asia Studies, University of California, Berkeley, 53–78.

Stapleton, K. (2022a) *The Modern City in Asia.* Cambridge: Cambridge University Press.

Stapleton, K. (2022b) The Rise of Municipal Government in Early Twentieth Century China: Local History, International Influence, and National Integration. *Twentieth-Century China* 47(1), 11–19.

Stelter, G. (2000) Rethinking the Significance of the City Beautiful Idea. In R. Freestone, ed., *Urban Planning in a Changing World: The Twentieth Century Experience.* London: E and FN Spon, 98–117.

Sulman, J. (1921) *An Introduction to Town Planning in Australia.* Sydney: William Applegate Gullick, Government Printer.

Sutcliffe, A. (1981) *Towards the Planned City: Germany, Britain, the United States and France, 1780–1914.* Oxford: Basil Blackwell.

Taylor, G. A. (1913) Canberra Saved. *Building* 13(74), 46.

Taylor, G. A. (1914) *Town Planning for Australia.* Sydney: Building.

Taylor, K. (2007) *Canberra: City in the Landscape.* Canberra: Halstead Press.

Taylor, M. and Kukina, I. (2018) Planning History in and of Russia and the Soviet Union. In C. Hein, ed., *The Routledge Handbook of Planning History.* London: Routledge, 192–207.

Thomas, M. J. (1978) City Planning in Soviet Russia (1917–1932). *Geoforum* 9, 269–277.

Tinio McKenna, R. (2017) *American Imperial Pastoral: The Architecture of US Colonialism in the Philippines.* Chicago: University of Chicago Press.

Toronto Guild of Art (1909) *Report on a Comprehensive Plan for Systematic Civic Improvements in Toronto.* Toronto: Toronto Guild of Civic Art.

Torre, S. (2002) Teaching Architectural History in Latin America: The Elusive Unifying Architectural Discourse. *Journal of the Society of Architectural Historians* 61(4), 549–558.

Torres, C. (2010) *The Americanization of Manila 1898–1921.* Quezon City: University of the Philippines Press.

Triggs, I. (1909) *Town Planning: Past, Present and Future.* London: Methuen.

Tsui, C. (2011) State Capacity in City Planning: The Reconstruction of Nanjing, 1927–1937. *Cross-Currents* 1(1), 1–43.

Tunnard, C. (1961) The City and Its Interpreters. *Journal of the American Institute of Planners* 27, 346–350.

Tyrrell, I. (2009), Reflections on the Transnational Turn in United States History: Theory and Practice. *Journal of Global History* 4(3), 453–474.

Union of Soviet Architects. (1935) *Moscow, General Plan for the Reconstruction of the City.* Moscow: Iskra Revolutsii Printshop No. 7.

Vale, L. (1992) *Architecture, Power, and National Identity.* New York: Routledge.

Van Nus, W. (1975) The Fate of City Beautiful Thought in Canada, 1893–1930. *Canadian Heritage* 12(1), 191–210.

Varias, A. (1955) Public Plazas and Open Areas in the City of Manila. *The Real Estate Digest* (July), 4–6.

Vernon, C. (2010a) Daniel Burnham's Philippines. The Landscape Architecture Dimension and Its Australian Import. *Espasyo* 3, 3–19.

Vernon, C. (2010b) Canberra: Where Landscape Is Pre-Eminent. In D. Gordon, ed., *Planning the Twentieth Century Capital Cities*. London: Routledge, 130–149.

Vernon, C. (2020) Manufacturing American Imperial Landscapes in the Tropics: Baguio and Balbao. In J. H. Hartman, ed., *Imperial Islands. Art, Architecture, and Visual Experience in the US Insular Empire after 1898*. Honolulu: University of Hawai'i Press, 161–185.

Waley, P. T. (2012) Japanese Cities in Chinese Perspective: Towards a Contextual, Regional Approach to Comparative Urbanism. *Urban Geography* 33(6), 812–828.

Waller, P. J. (1983) *Town, City, and Nation*. Oxford: Clarendon.

Ward, S. V. (2002) *Planning the Twentieth Century City*. Chichester: John Wiley and Sons.

Ward, S. V. (2005) A Pioneer 'Global Intelligence Corps'? The Internationalisation of Planning Practice, 1890–1939. *The Town Planning Review* 76(2), 119–141.

Ward, S. V. (2012) Soviet Communism and the British Planning Movement: Rational Learning or Utopian Imagining? *Planning Perspectives* 27(4), 499–524.

Ward, W. V. (2018) Planning Diffusion: Agents, Mechanisms, Networks, and Theories. In C. Hein, ed., *The Routledge Handbook of Planning History*. London: Routledge, 76–90.

Ward, S. V., Freestone, R., and Silver, C. (2011) The 'New' Planning History: Reflections, Issues and Directions. *The Town Planning Review* 82(3), 231–261.

Watanabe, S.-I. (2016) The Modern Planning History of East Asia: A Brief Guide from the Japanese Perspectives. *International Planning History Society Proceedings* 17(1), 13–18.

Webb, A. (1903) The Opening Address. *Journal of the Royal Institute of British Architects* 11, 1–11.

Webb, A. (1904) Gold Medal Speech. *Journal of the Royal Institute of British Architects* 12, 429–431.

Weber, R. and Crane, R. (2012) Planning as Scholarship: Origins and Prospects. In R. Weber and R. Crane, eds., *The Oxford Handbook of Urban Planning*. Oxford: Oxford University Press, 3–20.

Whyte, W. (2012) The 1910 Royal Institute of British Architects Conference: A Focus on International Town Planning. *Urban History* 39(1), 149–165.

Wilson, W. H. (1989) *The City Beautiful Movement*. Baltimore: The John Hopkins University Press.

Wolff, L. (1961) *Little Brown Brother: How the United States Purchased and Pacified the Philippine Islands at the Century's Turn*. New York: History Book Club.

Xu, Y. (2023) Historical Geographies of Japanese Colonial Urbanism. *Geography Compass* 17(3), 1–14.

Zhang, B. (2022) A Chinese Renaissance: Henry Killian Murphy and His Interpretation of Traditional Chinese Architecture. *Journal of Traditional Building, Architecture and Urbanism* 3, 312–324.

Zhu, J. (1998) Beyond Revolution: Notes on Contemporary Chinese Architecture. *AA Files* 35, 3–14.

Zubovich, K. (2024) *Making Cities Socialist*. Cambridge: Cambridge University Press.

Acknowledgements

The author wishes to express sincere gratitude to the Research Grants Council of Hong Kong for funding via the General Research Fund (e.g. project numbers 14408014 and 14604120) upon research for the Element was based, and to Mar Ticao and Shu Wang for assistance with primary source translation. He also wishes to offer sincere thankfulness to the referees for their constructive feedback regarding the original form of the text, and to the editors of the *Cambridge Elements in Global Urban History* book series for their guidance.

Cambridge Elements ☰

Global Urban History

Michael Goebel

Graduate Institute Geneva

Michael Goebel is the Pierre du Bois Chair Europe and the World and Associate Professor of International History at the Graduate Institute Geneva. His research focuses on the histories of nationalism, of cities, and of migration. He is the author of *Anti-Imperial Metropolis: Interwar Paris and the Seeds of Third World Nationalism* (2015).

Tracy Neumann

Wayne State University

Tracy Neumann is an Associate Professor of History at Wayne State University. Her research focuses on global and transnational approaches to cities and the built environment. She is the author of *Remaking the Rust Belt: The Postindustrial Transformation of North America* (2016) and of essays on urban history and public policy.

Joseph Ben Prestel

Freie Universität Berlin

Joseph Ben Prestel is an Assistant Professor (wissenschaftlicher Mitarbeiter) of history at Freie Universität Berlin. His research focuses on the histories of Europe and the Middle East in the nineteenth and twentieth centuries as well as on global and urban history. He is the author of *Emotional Cities: Debates on Urban Change in Berlin and Cairo, 1860–1910* (2017).

About the Series

This series proposes a new understanding of urban history by reinterpreting the history of the world's cities. While urban history has tended to produce single-city case studies, global history has mostly been concerned with the interconnectedness of the world. Combining these two approaches produces a new framework to think about the urban past. The individual titles in the series emphasize global, comparative, and transnational approaches. They deliver empirical research about specific cities, while also exploring questions that expand the narrative outside the immediate locale to give insights into global trends and conceptual debates. Authored by established and emerging scholars whose work represents the most exciting new directions in urban history, this series makes pioneering research accessible to specialists and non-specialists alike.

Cambridge Elements ≡

Global Urban History

A full series listing is available at: www.cambridge.org/EGUB

Printed in the United States
by Baker & Taylor Publisher Services